Pearson Revise

T0351587

Pearson Edexcel GCSE (9–1)

English Language 2.0

Revision Guide and Workbook

Series Editor: Harry Smith

Authors: Jane Cotter, Ben Cribbin and Katy Madgwick

Also available to support your revision:

Revise GCSE Study Skills Guide   9781292318875

The **Revise GCSE Study Skills Guide** is full of tried-and-trusted hints and tips for how to learn more effectively. It gives you techniques to help you achieve your best – throughout your GCSE studies and beyond!

Revise GCSE Revision Planner   9781292318868

The **Revise GCSE Revision Planner** helps you to plan and organise your time, step-by-step, throughout your GCSE revision. Use this book and wall chart to mastermind your revision.

For the full range of Pearson revision titles across KS2, 11+, KS3, GCSE, Functional Skills, AS/A Level and BTEC visit:
www.pearsonschools.co.uk/revise

Published by Pearson Education Limited, 80 Strand, London, WC2R 0RL.

www.pearsonschoolsandfecolleges.co.uk

Copies of official specifications for all Pearson qualifications may be found on the website: qualifications.pearson.com

Text and illustrations © Pearson Education Ltd 2022

Typeset and illustrated by Newgen KnowledgeWorks Pvt. Ltd., Chennai, India

Produced by Newgen Publishing UK

Cover illustration © Kamae Design Ltd

The rights of Jane Cotter, Ben Cribbin and Katy Madgwick to be identified as authors of this work have been asserted by them in accordance with the Copyright, Designs and Patents Act 1988.

First published 2022

25 24

10 9

British Library Cataloguing in Publication Data
A catalogue record for this book is available from the British Library

ISBN 978 1 292 42765 2

Acknowledgements
Material by Julie Hughes and David Grant is included in this book.

Text: P 5: Gould and Ewell: The Portland Transcript. 'Boy Lost' Volume XXIV. p212. Published in 1860 by Gould & Elwell. https://books.google.co.uk/books?id=RIccrvshng4C&pg=PA212&lpg=PA212&dq=boy+lost+he+had+black+eyes,+with+long+lashes+source&source=bl&ots=mr4goUf5PG&sig=ACfU3U28JmBcG1m1QdTY0zh2J8jJlxBpPw&hl=en&sa=X&ved=2ahUKEwibz8jC27j1AhWRT8AKHZaEBcgQ6AF6BAgqEAM#v=onepage&q=boy%20lost%20he%20had%20black%20eyes%2C%20with%20long%20lashes%20source&f=false Accessed: 10 Feb 2022; **P 6:** Haig, Matt. The Midnight Library. Canongate Books, © 2021; **P 7:** Young, Rosamund. The Secret Life of Cows, published by Faber & Faber, © 2017; **P 9:** Twain, Mark. Letters of Note by Mark Twain, published in 1905. https://news.lettersofnote.com/p/an-idiot-of-the-33rd-degree. Accessed: 10 Feb 2022; **P 10, 15, 16:** Haig, Matt. How to Stop Time. Canongate Books, © 2017 (7) **P 12, 68-74, 78, 170:** Dickens, Charles. Charles Dickens about the execution of the Mannings, Dickens' letter to The Times Nov. 13, 1849. https://www.charlesdickenspage.com/public-execution.html. Accessed. 10 Feb 2022 (10); **P 12, 60, 62, 63, 64, 64br, 65, 66, 169:** Bronte, Charlotte. Charlotte Bronte's letter to her father, written in 1851. https://aceyourexams.files.wordpress.com/2016/12/paper-2-source-a-charlotte-bronte.pdf Accessed: 10 Feb 2022 (10); **P 13:** Donoghue, Emma. Room, published by Pan Macmillan, © 2015, p17 6, Rashford, Marcus., You are A Champion, published by Pan Macmillan, © 2021; **P 14:** Orwell, George. Animal Farm published by E-Kitap Projesi & Cheapest Book, © 1945 (3); **P 17:** Sutherst, Thomas. 'Death and disease behind the counter.' Published by Kegan Paul, Trench & Co, Paternoster Square, 1884. https://archive.org/details/b28058252/page/4/mode/2up?q=refreshment. Accessed: 10 Feb 2022 (3); **P 21-24, 174:** Cumming, Ed. Sun, sea and silver service: what's it like crewing on a superyacht? Published by Guardian News & Media Limited, © 2014 (5); **P 21-24, 173:** Fitzgerald, F Scott The Great Gatsby. 1925. https://www.google.co.in/books/edition/The_Great_Gatsby/3IAUEAAAQBAJ?hl=en&gbpv=1. Accessed: 10 Feb 2022 (5); **P 33:** Williamson, Harriet. 'Unhappy at work? It's time to join 'The Great Resignation'. 03 NOV 2021 published by The Independent, © 2021. https://www.independent.co.uk/independentpremium/voices/the-great-resignation-covid-working-back-to-office-b1950557.html. Accessed: 10 Feb 2022; **P 46:** Obama, Barack. Remarks by the President in Address to the Nation on Immigration, Speech by Barack Obama. https://obamawhitehouse.archives.gov/the-press-office/2014/11/20/remarks-President-address-nation-immigration. Accessed: 10 Feb 2022 46; **P 46:** Shakespeare, William. Merchant of Venice, William Shakespeare published in 1600 46; **P 87, 88, 103-107, 172:** Rice Jones, D. 'In the Slums: pages from the note-book of a London Diocesan Home Missionary' by the Rev. D. Rice-Jones, 1844, pub James Nisbet & Co. https://www.victorianlondon.org/publications6/slums-01.htm Accessed: 10 Feb 2022 (9); **P 99-103, 171:** Beever, Susanna. 'Foodless, friendless, in our Streets; being a letter about Ragged Schools addressed to boys and girls.'' Published 1853 as a pamphlet. Public domain. British Library. https://www.bl.uk/collection-items/a-letter-about-ragged-schools#:~:text=This%20letter%20outlines%20some%20of,had%20by%20then%20become%20known.&text=%E2%80%9CFoodless%2C%20Friendless%2C%20in%20our,letter%20about%20Ragged%20Schools%2C%20etc. ACCESSED: 10 Feb 2022 (5); **P 139, 154, 155, 156, 160, 161, 163, 164, 175:** Martel, Yann. Extracts from 'Life of Pi'. Published by Canongate Books © 2003 and with additional permission from Westwood Creative Artists (10); **P 141, 157, 160-163, 176:** Dodge, Washington. Eyewitness account of the sinking of the Titanic by Washington Dodge, 1912. https://www.gilderlehrman.org/sites/default/files/inline-pdfs/t-07640_0.pdf [downloaded 24-11-21]. Accessed: 10 Feb 2022 (8)

Photos: 123RF: lightfieldstudios 134; **Alamy Stock Photo:** Pictorial Press Ltd 171; **Shutterstock:** Hein Nouwens 169, Alphaspir.it 134, Antonio Guillem 150, TORWAISTUDIO 150, Neotemlpars 37, Maria Jacobs 37.

Notes from the publisher
1. While the publishers have made every attempt to ensure that advice on the qualification and its assessment is accurate, the official specification and associated assessment guidance materials are the only authoritative source of information and should always be referred to for definitive guidance.

Pearson examiners have not contributed to any sections in this resource relevant to examination papers for which they have responsibility.

2. Pearson has robust editorial processes, including answer and fact checks, to ensure the accuracy of the content in this publication, and every effort is made to ensure this publication is free of errors. We are, however, only human, and occasionally errors do occur. Pearson is not liable for any misunderstandings that arise as a result of errors in this publication, but it is our priority to ensure that the content is accurate. If you spot an error, please do contact us at resourcescorrections@pearson.com so we can make sure it is corrected.

Contents

• •

A small bit of small print
Pearson Edexcel publishes Sample
Assessment Material and the
Specification on its website.
This is the official content and this
book should be used in conjunction
with it. The questions have been
written to help you practise every topic
in the book. Remember: the real exam
questions may not look like this.

Exams explained: Paper 1

The focus of Paper 1 is 19th-century non-fiction texts and transactional writing.

Non-fiction texts

You will study and analyse a wide range of functional 19th-century non-fiction texts, such as newspaper and magazine articles and reviews, instructional texts, speeches, journals and reference book extracts.

Section A: Reading – 40 marks (50% of Paper 1; 25% of the exam)

- ✓ You will read two short, thematically linked, previously unseen 19th-century non-fiction texts.
- ✓ You will answer six questions: three on each of the texts.
- ✓ The questions require a selection of short and extended responses.

 You should spend about 1 hour 10 minutes on Section A.

Transactional writing

You will explore and develop transactional writing skills, in the form of letters, articles, reports, speeches, reviews, formal emails or blogs.

Section B: Writing – 40 marks (50% of Paper 1; 25% of the exam)

- ✓ You will produce one piece of writing.
- ✓ You will choose between two writing questions.

 You should spend about 45 minutes on Section B.

Spoken language

As part of your exam, you will be assessed on your spoken language skills.

You will use spoken English to:

- present information and ideas
- listen and respond to questions.

This book focuses on your reading and writing assessments in Papers 1 and 2, but the skills covered here will help you in the preparation and structure of your spoken language assessment.

For more information about your spoken language assessment, speak to your teacher or visit the Pearson Edexcel GCSE English Language 2.0 website.

Now try this

Answer the following questions using information on this page.

1 What is the focus of Paper 1?

2 How long should you spend on Paper 1 Section A?

3 How many writing questions do you need to answer in Paper 1 Section B?

Exams explained: Paper 2

The focus of Paper 2 is contemporary texts and imaginative writing.

Contemporary texts

You will study and analyse a wide range of prose fiction and literary non-fiction, such as novels, autobiographies, biographies, memoirs, letters, speeches and travel writing. The texts will be from the 20th and 21st centuries.

Section A: Reading – 40 marks (50% of Paper 2; 25% of the exam)

- ☑ You will read two short, thematically linked, previously unseen texts.
- ☑ One text will be fiction and one will be literary non-fiction.
- ☑ One text will be from the 20th century and one will be from the 21st century.
- ☑ You will answer two questions on the first text, two questions on the second text and then two questions on both texts.

You should spend about 1 hour 10 minutes on Section A.

Imaginative writing

You will explore and develop imaginative writing skills.

Section B: Writing – 40 marks (50% of Paper 2; 25% of the exam)

- ☑ You will produce one piece of writing.
- ☑ You will choose between two writing questions.

You should spend about 45 minutes on Section B.

Understanding the exam questions

In this book, you can learn more about each type of exam question in Paper 1 and Paper 2.

For information on Paper 1 questions, look at pages 57 to 82. For Paper 2 questions, go to pages 113 to 138.

Assessment objectives

The exam questions will test you on different aspects of your reading and writing skills. In the Paper 1 and Paper 2 exam skills pages, you can see which assessment objectives are being tested in each question.

Now try this

1 What is the main focus of Paper 2?
2 How many reading questions do you need to answer in Paper 2 Section A?
3 How many writing questions do you need to answer in Paper 2 Section B?
4 How long should you spend on Paper 2 Section B?

Planning your exam time

Planning how you use your time in the exam is vital in helping you to do the best you can.

How much time do you have?

In each of Paper 1 and Paper 2, you will have **1 hour and 55 minutes** to complete all the questions. This means you have to read, plan, write and check your answers within this time. Base the time spent on each question on the number of marks available.

Information at the start of each section will also provide guidance as to how much time you should spend on each section: 1 hour 10 minutes for the Reading section and 45 minutes for the Writing section. However, it is up to you to effectively plan how to break this down between the questions.

> Remember to leave enough time for the Writing section – it is worth the same number of marks as the Reading section.

Reading: Using your time productively

① **Read the questions:** highlight key words to help you find the information you need when you read the sources.

② **Skim read:** concentrate on the headings, introductory sentence, first line of each paragraph and the conclusion to help focus on the main theme and ideas of each source.

③ **Read the detail:** now you have an idea of the themes, it is time to concentrate on all of the information to help you understand the purpose, context, genre, form and intended audience.

④ **Make notes:** highlight and annotate the key features of each source with short notes that relate to the question.

Paper 1 Non-fiction texts: Complete the table below by working out how much time you should spend on each question (P = Plan, W = Write, C = Check).

Question	Marks	Time
Section A: 1	4	
Section A: 2	6	
Section A: 3	8	
Section A: 4	4	
Section A: 5	6	
Section A: 6	12	
Section B: 7 or 8	40	

*Section A – 1 hour 10 minutes
*Section B – 45 minutes

Paper 2 Contemporary texts: Complete the table below by working out how much time you should spend on each question (P = Plan, W = Write, C = Check).

Question	Marks	Time
Section A: 1	1	
Section A: 2	6	
Section A: 3	1	
Section A: 4	10	
Section A: 5	6	
Section A: 6	16	
Section B: 7 or 8	40	

*Section A – 1 hour 10 minutes
*Section B – 45 minutes

Now try this

1 How many marks are available for each of Paper 1 and Paper 2?

2 How many marks are available for Section A and Section B in each paper?

Reading questions: an overview

Both Paper 1 and Paper 2 of GCSE English Language 2.0 include a Reading section (Section A). There will be different types of reading text in each paper.

Paper 1: Section A – Reading non-fiction texts

In this paper you will have two functional 19th-century non-fiction texts. These could include newspaper and magazine articles and reviews, instructional texts, speeches, journals and reference book extracts.

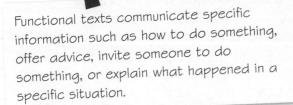

Functional texts communicate specific information such as how to do something, offer advice, invite someone to do something, or explain what happened in a specific situation.

You will be assessed on 19th-century texts – those written between 1800 and 1900. Though the language and format might not be the same as we use today, you will still need to identify themes, ideas and information.

Non-fiction reading – get ahead!

It is helpful to read a current newspaper article, website or blog every day. This will help you to identify language techniques and the transactional writing skills that writers use to inform, argue and persuade. You could think about how effective the writing is.

Make notes about the writer's **purpose**, **tone** and **point of view**.

Transactional writing includes a range of formats, such as letters, formal emails, speeches, reviews, blogs, articles or reports.

Paper 2: Section A – Reading contemporary texts

In Paper 2 you will have one fiction and one literary non-fiction text from the 20th and 21st centuries. These could include prose fiction and literary non-fiction, such as novels, autobiographies, biographies, memoirs, letters, speeches and travel writing.

Contemporary (adj) Existing, occurring or living in the present.

Contemporary texts reading – get ahead!

Reading a variety of contemporary fiction and literary non-fiction will help you become familiar with different literary genres (such as crime, horror, science fiction, romance and satire) and contemporary themes and issues.

When you are reading, start thinking about the **theme**, and **how** and **why** the writer has created particular **characters** and **atmospheres**.

Now try this

1 Which paper will cover 19th-century texts?
2 Give three examples of contemporary texts that you might be given.
3 Give three examples of fictional genres.

Skimming for the main idea

You have limited time in your exam, so it is important to skim read the text first to understand the main theme or idea. By quickly reading through the source, you should also be able to identify the purpose and content and the audience the writer was writing for.

Key features

1 The heading.

2 The first sentence of each paragraph.

3 The final sentence of the source.

Always read the introduction text on the exam paper which will give you information about what you are reading. Not all texts have headings.

This heading is short and suggests a child is missing. But is that really the case?

The final sentence draws together the theme of a mother whose child has grown up.

Always follow up your initial skim read with a further detailed reading to ensure you take in all the information.

BOY LOST

He had black eyes, with long lashes, red cheeks, and hair almost black and almost curly. He wore a crimson plaid jacket, with full trousers buttoned on, had a habit of whistling, and liked to ask questions. He was accompanied by a small black dog.

It is a long while now since he disappeared. I have a very pleasant house and much company. My guests say, 'Ah, it is pleasant to be here! Everything has such an orderly, put-away look – nothing about under foot, no dirt!'

But my eyes are aching for the sight of cut paper upon the floor; of tumbled-down card-houses; of wooden sheep and cattle; of tops and go-carts, yet these things used to fret me once.

I want to replace lost buttons. I want to obliterate mud stains, fruit stains, and paints of all colours. I want to be sitting by a little crib of evenings, when prattling voices are hushed, that mothers may sing their lullabies. They don't know their happiness then – those mothers. I didn't. All these things I called [responsibilities] once.

A manly figure stands before me now. He is taller than I, has thick black whiskers, and wears a frock coat, billowy shirt, and cravat. He has just come from college. He calls me mother, but I am rather unwilling to own him. He stoutly declares that he is my boy, and says he will prove it. He brings me a small pair of trousers and asks me if I didn't make them for him. And I see it all as plain as if it were written in a book. My little boy is lost.

Now try this

Summarise the main idea of the article in one sentence.

Annotating the texts

Annotating is making notes or short comments on a source or on parts of a source that you can then develop in your response.

How to annotate

You can highlight, underline or circle key information in the source text. Make sure all of the text is still clear for you to read and refer to.

- ✓ Focus on the key words in the question.
- ✓ Check which part of the source you need to refer to in your answer.
- ✓ Use the correct technical language.

In your revision for Paper 1 and Paper 2, practise highlighting important information in the sources that you can use to support and provide evidence for your answer. Once you have done this, make short notes on technique and the effect of the language used.

Annotating for an exam question

It's important to read exam questions carefully before annotating. Read the question, text and student annotations below to see how the student picks relevant information from the text in preparation for writing their answer.

> 4   How does the writer try to interest and inform the reader?

You should include:

- ✓ the writer's use of language
- ✓ the writer's use of structure
- ✓ the effect on the reader.

Use examples from the whole text and relevant subject terminology.

Extract from The Midnight Library *by Matt Haig*

Nora walked onto the stage.

At first she couldn't see the faces because the lights were pointing towards her, and beyond that glare, everything seemed like darkness. Except for a mesmerising milky way of camera flashes and phone torches.

She could hear them though.

Human beings when there's enough of them together acting in total unison become something else. The collective roar made her think of another kind of animal entirely. It was at first kind of threatening, as if she was Hercules facing the many-headed Hydra who wanted to kill him ...

Short sentence creates impact.

Imagery helps reader to visualise the scene.

Reference to senses introduces the visual of a loud crowd. Short sentence creates impact by the contrast with the loss of sense of sight.

Use of verb 'roar' indicates that people have come together to create an animal. Simile reinforces the character's feeling of fear.

Now try this

Read the extract on the right and highlight and annotate words or phrases in response to the example Paper 2 question above.

Note that the text in your exam will be longer than this example.

Extract from Room *by Emma Donoghue*

While Bath is running, Ma gets Labyrinth and Fort down from the top of Wardrobe. We've been making Labyrinth since I was two, she's all toilet roll insides taped together in tunnels that twist lots of ways. Bouncy Ball loves to get lost in the Labyrinth and hide, I have to call out to him and shake her and turn her sideways and upside down before he rolls out, whew.

6

Explicit information and ideas

Paper 1 and Paper 2 will both test you on your understanding of a writer's theme or topic. You will have to answer short questions to demonstrate that you can identify the correct answers from the explicit information you are given.

What are explicit information and ideas?

Identifying explicit information and ideas means you have to look for something that is clearly stated in the text. You don't need to look for hidden meanings.

You will not have to explain your answer – just identify the correct answers. You may need to find short quotations or paraphrase (put into your own words) what is obviously there.

Explicit (*adjective*)

Stated clearly and in detail, leaving no room for confusion or doubt: 'the arrangement had not been made explicit'.

Synonyms: clear, direct, plain, obvious, straightforward, clear-cut, crystal clear, clearly expressed, easily understandable, blunt.

Looking for explicit information and ideas

Read 1-mark questions carefully before going to the text to find the explicit information. The question may tell you which lines to look at. If it doesn't, then refer to the whole text.

These questions are about *The Secret Life of Cows*.

> From lines 1–9, identify why the writer may not see a group of cattle for some time. **(1 mark)**
>
> work allocation

This type of question is asking you to find 'explicit' information. The answer is directly in the source material.

> Apart from by their voices, identify **one** way the writer thinks sheep may recognise human beings. **(1 mark)**
>
> their looks

TOP TIP

For the 1-mark question parts on **both papers**, keep your answers short – don't waste time writing in full sentences.

21st

Extract from The Secret Life of Cows

One of the nicest attributes a cow can possess is a good memory. I say this from the human perspective of course, though I dare say a good memory is also useful to a cow. 5
Sometimes work allocation might prevent one of us from seeing a particular group of cattle for several weeks, although someone else in the family might see that 10
same group each day. No matter how long the parting, we are always individually remembered.
Cows have their favourite people as well as vice versa. Sheep also 15
have long and accurate memories. It seems now to be an accepted fact that they can recognise at least fifty of their individual companions.
From experience I conclude that 20
they remember all of the human beings they have ever known. The evidence I have seen indicates that they recognise us by our voices but perhaps they notice what we 25
look like, how we walk or even our height.

Now try this

Read the extract and answer these questions.

1 List **three** ways animals recognise humans.
2 How many companions can a sheep recognise?
3 What does the writer suggest is useful to a cow?

Implicit information and ideas

In addition to explicit information, in Paper 1 and Paper 2 you will have to identify implicit information.

What does it mean?

In some texts you will have to interpret what the writer is implying or suggesting – you will have to find the **implicit** meaning. This is sometimes called **making an inference**. Not all of the information you need will be clear (**explicit**).

Implicit (*adjective*) Suggested though not directly expressed: 'comments seen as implicit criticism of the children'.

Synonyms: implied, indirect, inferred, understood, hinted, suggested, deducible.

Implicit meaning in fiction

Writers use implicit meaning to draw the reader in and engage them. By not telling the reader everything, the writer allows the reader to feel that they have formed their own opinion or drawn their own conclusion about a scene, character or setting. For example, the reader doesn't need to be told explicitly that the opening scene is set in a busy bus or railway station:

> Throngs of people moved in all directions, the bored impatience of commuters mingling with the wide-eyed excitement of tourists and day trippers.

Implicit meaning in non-fiction and literary non-fiction

In non-fiction writing, implicit meaning can be an effective tool. Though some writers may choose to use a clear and explicit heading or opening statement, others may gradually build their viewpoint or argument. This works in the same way as implicit meaning in fiction – by drawing the reader in and persuading them to agree.

Using inference to find implicit meaning

In this example, inference is used to generate ideas about the character's childhood.

Didn't go to school.

Suggests he lived on a farm or in a rural area.

Never knew another way of life.

> No playgrounds or books for me. As soon as I could walk, it was into the yard feeding the hens and then the fields as I grew. I never questioned it, never thought to. My brothers had done the same, my father and uncles before us.

Now try this

Read lines 1–9 of Paper 1 Text 2 on page 170.

Then identify:

1 a piece of explicit information

2 an implicit idea.

The writer's viewpoint

In texts, identifying the writer's viewpoint will help you effectively comment on how they express their ideas in their writing.

Viewpoint

A viewpoint is the writer's attitude and opinion on a particular subject. Most texts reveal something about the writer's viewpoint. But in some texts the writer gives the facts as clearly as possible without revealing their own viewpoint. These texts are unbiased.

You will need to determine if the viewpoint is positive or negative.

When discussing a writer's viewpoint, you are looking at their opinions about, and attitude towards, a topic.

> Newspapers, letters, websites and blogs often reveal details about the writer's opinions. This means not all of it is fact. A viewpoint is not a fact and there may be some bias (favouring one perspective) in the writing.

Identifying a viewpoint

The introduction: the writer states their viewpoint immediately: they are baffled by what they have read. They cannot understand how a letter and an advertisement can be written by the same person and convey this with mockery.

Viewpoint: the writer clearly expresses their disgust at what they have read in the advertisement and towards the person who wrote it.

Conclusion: the writer concludes their disapproval with dismissal and pity. Their contempt is obvious.

Nov. 20. 1905

Dear Sir,

Your letter is an insoluble puzzle to me. The handwriting is good and exhibits considerable character, and there are even traces of intelligence in what you say, yet the letter and the accompanying advertisements profess to be the work of the same hand.

The person who wrote the advertisement is without a doubt the most ignorant person now alive on the planet; also without doubt he is an idiot, an idiot of the 33rd degree, and scion of an ancestral possession of idiots stretching back to the Missing Link. It puzzles me to make out how the same hand could have constructed your letter and your advertisements.

Puzzles fret me, puzzles annoy me, puzzles exasperate me; and always, for a moment, they arouse in me an unkind state of mind toward the person who has puzzled me. A few moments from now my resentment will have faded and passed and I shall probably even be praying for you.

Adieu, adieu, adieu!

Mark Twain

Now try this

Give an example of how the writer uses repetition effectively to express their viewpoint.

Inference

In Paper 1 and Paper 2 you will need to make inferences when a question asks you about the feelings, thoughts, views and actions of the writer, or the people or places they are writing about. Remember, inference is about working out what the writer is implying (suggesting).

What is the writer implying?

It's a warm place.

Suggests the woman is unconscious or dead.

Suggests that the narrator is feeling guilty.

Extract from How to Stop Time *by Matt Haig*

Chandrika Seneviratne was lying under a tree, in the shade, a hundred metres or so behind the temple. Ants crawled over her wrinkled face. Her eyes were closed. I heard a rustling in the leaves above and looked up to see a monkey staring down at me with judging eyes.

Using inference

Writers often suggest information rather than giving it directly. Readers can infer meaning from patterns, themes, language choices or what is unsaid. Consider:

- ✔ your own impression after reading the text
- ✔ the clues the writer has provided
- ✔ whether your idea fits with the whole text
- ✔ the evidence you can use to support your impression.

TOP TIP

- Always refer to evidence from the source you are given.
- Always comment on what can be inferred from the evidence.
- Aim to develop the point with additional comments and evidence from the source.

This is an example of a Paper 2 question where you could consider inference:

> 4   How does the writer try to interest and engage the reader?
> You should include:
> - the writer's use of language
> - the writer's use of structure
> - the effect on the reader.
>
> Use examples from the whole text and relevant subject terminology.

TOP TIP

Bullet points in this example of a Paper 2 question are a useful guide to help you structure your response.

 Now try this

Read this short extract from *How to Stop Time*, then answer the question.

Extract from How to Stop Time *by Matt Haig*

Hendrich was back in Los Angeles. He hadn't lived there since the 1920s so he assumed it was pretty safe to do so and that no one was alive who would remember him from before.
He had a large house in Brentwood … Brentwood was perfect for him. A geranium-scented land of large houses tucked behind high fences and walls and hedges, where the streets were free from pedestrians and everything, even the trees, looked perfect to the point of sterile.

What impression of Hendrich do you get from this extract? Include two points and use a short quotation to support each point and back up your answer.

Connotations

A connotation is where a writer's choice of words suggests meanings or ideas in addition to explicitly describing something. Connotations can add atmosphere to writing and draw the reader in with emotional associations. Considering what words or phrases suggest is another way that you can explore a writer's choice of language.

Language choice

The three sentences below all have similar literal meanings, but the connotations of the nouns and verbs used let you know the writer's actual feelings about the comfort of the weather.

1 The warm air wrapped around me.

2 The balmy atmosphere enveloped me.

3 The gentle breeze swathed me.

Evaluating and commenting on the **connotations** of the language in a text can help you to write about the **atmosphere** that is created, or about the **attitude** of the writer.

Connotations in context

Words can mean different things depending on what comes before and after them in a text. Consider the whole text in order to understand the words correctly – in context – and recognise their connotations.

Context (*noun*) The parts of something written or spoken that immediately precede and follow a word or passage and clarify its meaning.

Connotations of names

Some writers may pick names of places or characters that have connotations for the reader. For example, in his novel *Animal Farm*, George Orwell gives animals names that reflect their characters: Napoleon is the powerful leader; Squealer is the sneaky telltale; Boxer is strong and determined.

Now try this

What are the connotations of these words?

red   skull   lion

P–E–E paragraphs

P–E–E is a simple technique that you can use to plan your answers. The structure will help to make your writing clearer and more organised. P–E–E is particularly useful when answering questions that ask you to:

- **comment** on language and structure
- **evaluate** a text
- **compare** texts.

Point–Evidence–Explain in practice

1 Make your **point**.

2 Give **evidence** to support it.

3 **Explain** how the evidence supports the point.

> The writer uses... The article focuses on...

> For example,... The writer describes...

> This suggests... The writer is implying...

> How does the writer use language to interest and inform the reader?
>
> You should include:
> - the writer's use of language
> - the effect on the reader.

Look at this example of how a student uses Point–Evidence–Explain to answer the above question:

> **(Point)** The writer opens with the topic, immediately hinting at the awe of her experience. **(Evidence)** For instance, the reference to 'second time' straightaway tells the reader that **(Explain)** the writer has been before and so there must be something very interesting to see there.
>
> **(Point)** The writer helps the reader realise that this is a unique experience by describing the Palace with adjectives **(Evidence)** 'vast, strange, new' and by detailing the marvels of the exhibits: 'the most gorgeous work of the goldsmith and silversmith'. **(Explain)** By writing in this way, the reader is struck by the writer's breathless excitement, leaving the reader wanting to know more.

Extract from a text by Charlotte Brontë. Full text on page 169.

> Yesterday I went for the second time to the Crystal Palace. It is a wonderful place – vast, strange, new, and impossible to describe. Its grandeur does not consist in one thing, but in the unique assemblage of all things. Whatever human industry has created, you find there, from the great compartments filled with railway engines and boilers, with mill-machinery in full work, with splendid carriages of all kinds, with harness of every description – to the glass-covered and velvet-spread stands loaded with the most gorgeous work of the goldsmith and silversmith ...

The paragraph opens with a detailed point that addresses the question.

The adverbial 'for instance' shows clearly that evidence will be used, and a quotation is given.

Short quotations are effectively embedded within the sentence.

The evidence is then explained in detail with a comment on the effect of the language on the reader.

Now try this

Read the extract from Paper 1 Text 2 by Charles Dickens. Plan a P–E–E answer to this question:

How does the writer use language to present their point of view?

> The horrors of the gibbet and of the crime which brought the wretched murderers to it, faded in my mind before the atrocious bearing, looks and language, of the assembled spectators.

Word classes

In your exam you will be asked to comment on the writer's use of language. A good place to begin is to consider how they use different types of words to describe or provide more information.

Nouns

These words are used for people, places, ideas and objects.

- People: dancer, girl, grandfather, Lucy.
- Places: country, city, Wembley.
- Ideas: sadness, belief, honesty, friendship.
- Objects: shoe, window, car, brush.

When nouns indicate an idea, they are called abstract nouns.

Pronouns – I, me, she, they, theirs, our, etc. – can replace nouns.

Adjectives

Adjectives are used to describe nouns. They make descriptions more interesting.

> The *graceful* dancer floated across the *illuminated* stage.

Adjectives joined with a hyphen are called **compound adjectives.**

> Jude has a *part-time* job in the city.

To show degrees of difference, adjectives can also be **comparative**, such as warmer, lighter. These can then be extended to be **superlatives** such as warmest, lightest.

Verbs

This word class is used to describe actions – physical or mental:

- Physical: cough, run, walk, whistle.

> Callum *is playing* cricket in the County League.

- Mental: think, perceive, imagine, hope.

> The school *is considering* its policy on uniform requirements.

Adverbs

Adverbs give more information about the verb that is used and tell you how the action is being done.

> The man coughed *loudly.*

Usually, adverbs are often made by adding *-ly* to an adjective.

> quick → quickly
> slow → slowly
> near → nearly

Now try this

1 Read this short extract. In the text, underline the nouns and circle the verbs.

Extract from You Are a Champion *by Marcus Rashford*

For as long as I can remember, all I've wanted to do is play. It doesn't matter what position I'm playing in, what the weather's like or who the opponent is, if you give me a chance to play, that's what I'm going to do.

2 Write a short passage describing making breakfast. Use nouns, verbs, adjectives and adverbs to make it interesting for the reader.

Figurative language

Figurative language is language that goes further than the obvious meaning of the individual words by using language devices (figures of speech). Understanding how writers use language devices to convey emotion or create atmosphere can help you improve your own writing. When commenting on a piece of writing, give the name of the language device used together with the effect it has on the reader.

Metaphor

This device is a direct comparison of one thing with another. Metaphors help the reader create a visual picture in their mind.

> The museum was a **key**, unlocking the secrets of time.

Here the museum is compared to a key.

The metaphor suggests it is a source of knowledge and 'unlocking the secrets of time' implies access to history.

Simile

This is a comparison of one thing with another. It uses 'like' or 'as' to help create a vivid image.

> She was as **busy** as a **bee**.

Here, this simple example creates a picture of someone moving quickly, doing many things.

> She was as **slow** as a **snail**.

Here, the simile creates an image of someone unhurried and sluggish.

Personification

This device gives human characteristics to something that is non-human.

> The wind (bellowed) around the house.

Here the wind is personified by suggesting it is shouting.

> The wind (whispered) around the house.

Here the wind is personified by suggesting it is talking quietly.

The change in word creates two very different atmospheres: the first is angry and loud, and the second is gentle and soft.

Examples in literature

In *Animal Farm* by George Orwell, the writer's descriptive language has an immediate effect on the reader by setting the atmosphere and using strong imagery.

Metaphor: the writer uses this device to describe the reaction to events in the book.

> A wave of rebelliousness ran through the countryside.

Simile: the writer compares the hardness of the frozen soil to that of iron, making it impossible to plough.

> In January there came bitterly hard weather. The earth was like iron and nothing could be done in the fields.

Personification: the writer's use of the word 'dancing' personifies the lantern:

> With the ring of light from his lantern dancing from side to side, he lurched across the yard...

Now try this

Write your own example of a metaphor, simile and personification.

Creation of character

For Paper 2 you may need to comment on the way a writer has used language and structure to create a particular impression of a character. Read the extracts below from *How to Stop Time* by Matt Haig.

Character through action

Think about what the character is doing.

> I was standing outside her door.
>
> I had knocked and waited and knocked again.
>
> The watchman, who I had passed at the corner of the street, was now approaching.
>
> 'It is a marked house, lad.'
>
> 'Yes, I know that.'
>
> 'You must not go in there… It is unsafe.'
>
> I held out my hand. 'Stand back. I am cursed with it too.'

Identify action words – verbs and adverbs. Reference these with explicit links to what they tell you about the character.

Here, the action verbs, 'knocked' and 'waited' create the impression of determination. This tells us the character is strong-willed and resolute.

The action followed by the short sentence 'Stand back' hints at the drama and serious urgency of the situation.

Character through description

Think about how the writer describes the character.

> He was a long way off but he was easy to recognise. He was as large as a haystack. He was walking along with his arms hanging by his sides in a strange fashion, as if they were dead things attached to him.

Look out for describing words and figurative language devices.

The narrator tells us the character is easily identifiable – even from a distance.

The use of a simile creates a vivid image of an immense man.

The detail of his movements and comparison to 'dead things' alert the reader to the fact that something isn't right.

Character through dialogue

What do we learn from what a character says?

> 'I don't know.'
>
> 'That is a lie.'
>
> 'I can't tell you who he is.'
>
> 'He said your mother was a witch. What was his meaning?'
>
> 'He must be confused. He must have mistaken me for somebody else.'
>
> Her green eyes glared at me, alive with quiet fury.
>
> 'Do you take me for a fool, Tom Smith?'

Look out for additional details about the character in the dialogue.

The narrator has been caught out on a lie. He is hiding something. He is beginning to panic to cover up the truth.

The short sentences hint at the anger of the situation.

Now try this

Read lines 1–22 of Text 1 on page 173. Write a sentence to explain what impression you get of the character Gatsby.

Creation of atmosphere

You may need to think about how writers have used language and/or structure devices in order to create atmosphere. Sometimes this is called the 'mood' or 'tone' of a text. You may also be asked to comment on how a writer presents a setting (scene).

Personification of gossip makes it seem vital and valuable.

Simile – creates a sense of annoyance and irritation.

One-word sentence creates impact.

Alliteration – reinforces the idea of a crowded, bustling area.

Extract from How to Stop Time *by Matt Haig*

Gossip.

Gossip lived. It wasn't just a currency, it had a life.

Stories buzzed and hummed and circulated like gadflies in the air, hovering amid the stench of sewage and the clatter of carts.

Taking an overview

Once you have identified what techniques the writer has used, consider their connotations and the effect they have. How do they work together to create a mood?

This is called taking an 'overview' and will help demonstrate your full understanding of the source text or extract.

The main mood of the extract above is one of a busy, bustling, lively, crowded place.

TOP TIP

When responding to a question about the writer's techniques, start with the overview you have identified. Introduce your findings with phrases such as these:

• Overall, the writer suggests…

• Essentially, the writer creates…

• The overall tone of the extract is…

Atmosphere can be created through:

• setting

• characters

• dialogue

• objects

• actions.

Now try this

Read the extract from *How to Stop Time*.

1 Identify the techniques used and comment on their effect or connotations.

2 What overall mood or tone is created by the writer?

Extract from How to Stop Time *by Matt Haig*

It is strange how close the past is, even when you imagine it to be so far away. Strange how it can jump out of a sentence and hit you. Strange how every object or word can house a ghost.

16

Whole text structure: non-fiction

The overall structure of non-fiction texts can be used by writers to develop their ideas. Structure can help to create a particular tone, organise a text for a particular purpose or manipulate the reader's response. You should be aware of structure also when you write your own texts in the Section B Writing sections of each paper.

Headings

Headings can be used to both engage the reader and present the writer's viewpoint.

Here, the heading gives a stark warning about the dangers of working in a shop.

Opening

In this example, the writer starts by identifying the long hours associated with shop work and the time spent standing.

> **DEATH AND DISEASE BEHIND THE COUNTER**
> The most exhausting incident of shop work is the long, long, standing. I do not contend that it would be either possible or convenient for assistants to sit and discharge their duties, …

Any text opening needs to engage the reader, setting the scene or introducing the main point.

Development

The body of the text has to hold the reader's initial engagement.

A writer can achieve this by:

- altering the tone
- introducing an alternative argument
- developing an argument
- providing more explanation (e.g. facts; opinions, expert evidence).

The writer develops their argument, that rest is beneficial to both workers and customers.

> The view in which standing is regarded by shopkeepers themselves is plainly apparent from the solicitude they show for the comfort of their customers by providing seats for purchasers. It is undoubtedly more agreeable to sit and select what is required than to stand, but so far as there is an actual and pressing need of rest as between the assistants and purchasers, it appears to me that the seats are at the wrong side of the counter. A little more solicitude in this direction for the young men and women behind the counter would, I am sure, not only be profitable to the employers, but would be appreciated substantially by considerate purchasers.

Conclusion

Effective endings leave readers with a lasting impression. Ending styles can include:

- vivid images
- advice
- perspectives
- calls to action
- rhetorical questions
- a summary of the main points made.

Here, the writer asks for the reader's empathy and own experience of exhaustion and compares this to the historical torture of witches. Though there is no direct call to action, there is no presentation of alternative views. The writer holds firm that change is needed.

> The wasting fatigue resulting from standing scarcely needs any illustration, for almost everyone knows from experience that there are few more painful sensations than the feeling of complete exhaustion which prostrates the whole system after even a comparatively short period of standing. … We know that incessant walking for twenty-four hours was considered one of the most unbearable tortures to which witches in former times were subjected for the purpose of compelling them to their own guilt, and that few of them could hold out for twelve hours.

Now try this

Name **three** features of structure.

Identifying sentence types

You may need to comment on the types of sentences a writer uses to create effects and how they can influence the reader's response to the text.

Single-clause sentences

These are also called simple sentences. They have only one clause and provide one piece of information about an event or action.

They contain a subject and one verb. For example:

The dog barked.

He yelled.

She went to town.   *This is the verb.*

A clause is a group of words containing a subject and a verb.

Multi-clause sentences

These are sometimes referred to as compound or complex sentences. They have more than one clause and have two or more verbs. For example:

After we have eaten lunch, we are going to take the dog for a walk.

Multi-clause sentences may contain coordinate and/or subordinate clauses.

Minor sentences

These are not full sentences. Without a verb they are grammatically incomplete. For example:

Yes, sir.

Coordinate clauses

Clauses are coordinate if neither clause depends on the other. For example:

The hounds were howling and the cats were hissing.

Each of these clauses are equal.

Here, the two clauses are joined with conjunctions such as 'and' (as in the example), 'but' and 'or'.

See page 19 for information on the effects that different sentence types have on the reader.

Subordinate clauses

A subordinate clause is dependent on the main clause to make sense. For example:

This is the main clause.

The hounds howled until she returned.

This is the subordinate clause. The clause 'until she returned' makes no sense on its own.

Here you can see how two clauses can be joined with conjunctions such as 'until' (as in the example), 'although' and 'if'.

A subordinate clause can come after or before the main clause. For example:

Until she returned, the hounds howled.

Now try this

What kind of sentences are these? How do you know?

1 Seventeen.

2 They went swimming and had lunch.

3 She is a coach.

4 Because the children were screaming, her ears were ringing.

18

Commenting on sentence types

Sentence structure can provide as much impact on the reader as the writer's language choice.

Short sentences

Short sentences are often found in texts for younger children. They consist of a single main clause with a verb.

However, they can also be used effectively in writing to express an opinion, or to convey tension in creative writing.

> Who's there?

The simple and short question sentence immediately suggests drama.

Long sentences

In a longer, complex sentence, one clause is dependent on another clause for meaning. These are more likely to be found in writing aimed at an adult audience.

> The trunk, hidden away in the corner of the attic for decades, was covered in dust and locked by a key lost long ago.

Used effectively, these sentences can be descriptive and draw the reader in to the scene.

Long and short sentences

Short, single-clause sentences can be used for dramatic effect, when following a longer, multi-clause sentence.

> Some people believe in rising at dawn; eating green; intensive yoga sessions; hours of meditation; no TV and sleeping a full eight hours. I do not.

Placing a short sentence after a detailed longer sentence is also an effective way to summarise or contrast the content that comes before it.

For information on single- and multi-clause sentences, see page 18.

Effects of sentences

These sentences can also be effective:

- **questions and rhetorical questions** (e.g. Why me?)
- **exclamations** (e.g. Congratulations! It's a girl!)
- **commands** (e.g. Vote for your school council today.)
- **statements** (e.g. The bus is always late.)

Consider the effect of each of these examples and why the writer has presented their sentences in this way.

Sentences and punctuation

Punctuation is important for accuracy. It can also be used to create a particular effect.

> What now? That was the first clue: this job wasn't going to be easy.

The use of a short question sentence shows the narrator's unease in the situation.

Now try this

1 What sentence type(s) might a writer use to build tension?
2 What sentence type(s) might a writer use to describe a serene country scene?
3 What sentence type(s) might a writer use to describe a fast-paced scene?
4 Increase the impact of the passage below by adding a simple sentence at the end.

Volunteering is available to everyone and provides you with opportunities to make friends, be part of a community and help.

Synthesising two texts

In Paper 2 you will need to compare and summarise two texts. You will look at two writers' ideas, points of view and how they present both of these things. Synthesising and comparing two texts can be challenging, so focus on an area of structure or language to give a clear response.

The texts

To 'synthesise' means to bring together information from different sources into something new. For Paper 2 Questions 5 and 6, you will need to write about the similarities or differences between two texts.

You should:

- make statements about clear similarities or differences between the sources
- select details from both sources to use as evidence
- make clear inferences about both sources.

- Read the question and underline the key words to identify the focus.
- Skim read both texts, underlining in both any relevant evidence.

See page 126 for more on finding similarities for Question 5. See pages 129–130 for comparing ideas and perspectives about a theme for Question 6.

Direct comparisons

Make direct comparisons of an element of the texts. For example, by focusing on one language feature or its effect in the first text, you can then compare it to a similar feature or effect in the second text.

You can explore the differences by writing about the structure of the texts, or their tones and the language features used to create them.

Linking words and phrases

Adverbials are useful language tools that you can use to indicate the development of your response.

You can highlight a similarity with adverbials such as: likewise, equally, as well, similarly.

To highlight differences, you can use words such as: alternatively, on the other hand, in contrast, however.

TOP TIP

For more on adverbials, refer to page 45.

Make sure you understand what each text is about before you start planning your comparison.

Always clearly state which text you are referring to:

- Text 1 has...
- In Text 2,...

Comparing writers' ideas and points of view

For comparison questions:

- remember to highlight key words in the question to help you focus your response
- refer to both sources
- identify the key similarities and differences
- identify language devices
- think about how ideas and perspectives are presented in each text.

Look at pages 24 and 25 for more on comparing language and structure.

Now try this

1 Give one example of an adverbial you can use to highlight a similarity between two texts.
2 Give one example of an adverbial you can use to highlight a difference between two texts.

Comparing ideas

When comparing two sources, you will need to compare the main ideas and themes that the writers are presenting.

Comparing ideas

1 Skim read both of the full sources to identify the main idea of each paragraph.

2 Use language and structural comparisons to explain how the writers present their ideas.

3 Make sure you clearly state which source you are referring to. You can refer simply to 'Text 1' and 'Text 2'.

Extract from The Great Gatsby: *lines 11–14 of the full text extract on page 173.*

At least once a fortnight a corps of caterers came down with several hundred feet of canvas and enough colored lights to make a Christmas tree of Gatsby's enormous garden. On buffet tables, garnished with glistening hors-d'oeuvre, spiced baked hams crowded against salads of harlequin designs and pastry pigs and turkeys bewitched to a dark gold.

Extract from travel writing: lines 4–9 of the full text extract on page 174.

Still, nobody pays much attention as I wander up to the first of these beasts, the motor yacht Katara. It is thought to have cost around $300m. You don't spend that much on a boat not to have anyone notice. Crew in white shirts and khaki shorts swarm over its decks, making final preparations to the scene. Everything is immaculate. Glasses and cutlery are laid on tables. Sun-loungers are set out on the teak transom, towels rolled in tight cylinders. On the top deck a helicopter waits. It all gleams in the sunshine.

Similarity in the main idea: both texts describe the decadence and extravagance of the wealthy and the expected perfection of the staff that work for them.

Similarity in language: both writers use vivid descriptions and long sentences.

Difference in language and effect: *The Great Gatsby* is full of figurative language and long descriptions; it paints a clear picture of the lavish existence of Gatsby. Conversely, the travel writing uses short, sharp sentences – highlighting the precision of the yacht's presentation. Minimal use is made of figurative language, but where it is used ('Crew in white shirts and khaki shorts swarm over its decks'), it enhances the image of how busy the people are and the painstaking attention to detail.

See page 22 for detail on comparing writers' perspectives.

Now try this

Read both texts on pages 175 and 176. Give one further example of similarity in the theme and idea of the texts.

Comparing perspective

When comparing two sources, you will need to compare the perspective (point of view) that the writers are presenting.

What are writers' perspectives?

The source texts in Paper 2 will be linked. As you skim read through each source looking for the main idea, identify how the writer feels about this theme. Some writers will immediately state a perspective, others may introduce it later and build on it throughout the text.

> **Perspective** (*noun*) A particular attitude towards or way of reading something; a point of view.
>
> *Synonyms*: outlook, attitude, view, position, stand, feelings about an idea.

> Remember that a writer's perspective can depend on the context in which they are writing.

Extract from Text 1, The Great Gatsby: lines 1–6 of the full text extract on page 173.

There was music from my neighbor's house through the summer nights. On week-ends his Rolls-Royce became an omnibus, bearing parties to and from the city, between nine in the morning and long past midnight, while his station wagon scampered like a brisk yellow bug to meet all trains. And on Mondays eight servants including an extra gardener toiled all day with mops and scrubbing-brushes and hammers and garden-shears, repairing the ravages of the night before.

Extract from Text 2, travel writing: lines 19–23 of the full text extract on page 174.

Culinary choices are only the start of the potential tensions on board. Compared with the five-star hotel standard of the guest state-rooms, the crew accommodation is usually cramped and shared. Crew will wake up to serve breakfast and then stay until the last guest has gone to bed, meaning days can be up to 20 hours. There are no weekends at sea. On superyachts the owner is God, followed quickly by the captain and the guests.

Difference in perspective

The texts will usually present different perspectives on a similar theme, but read them carefully to check.

In the above text extracts, both writers present the lives of the rich through the eyes of their hard-working staff – they have a similar main idea. However, in Text 1 the writer talks about the drivers and servants whereas, in Text 2, the writer presents the perspective of an outsider observing.

When comparing perspectives use:

- your overview paragraph to introduce the comparison of perspectives
- words such as 'feels' or 'suggests' to show you understand the writer's perspective
- signposting to introduce further detail, e.g. 'By contrast,…', 'To communicate this,…'.

Now try this

Read both texts on pages 175 and 176. Give one example with evidence showing how the writers present their ideas and perspectives about the lives of the rich.

Comparing structure

When comparing two sources in Paper 2, you will need to look at how writers structure their writing to convey their ideas.

Comparing structure

Consider the aspects of structure in the diagram. Look for any similarities or differences in how the two writers use structure. Consider what effect these have on the reader.

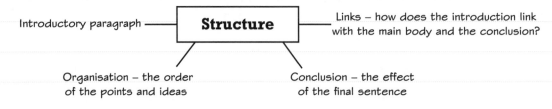

Introductory paragraph — **Structure** — Links – how does the introduction link with the main body and the conclusion?

Organisation – the order of the points and ideas

Conclusion – the effect of the final sentence

 20th

Extract from Text 1: The Great Gatsby: lines 11–16 of the full text extract on page 173.

At least once a fortnight a corps of caterers came down with several hundred feet of canvas and enough colored lights to make a Christmas tree of Gatsby's enormous garden. On buffet tables, garnished with glistening hors-d'oeuvre, spiced baked hams crowded against salads of harlequin designs and pastry pigs and turkeys bewitched to a dark gold. In the main hall a bar with a real brass rail was set up, and stocked with gins and liquors and with cordials so long forgotten that most of his female guests were too young to know one from another.

The opening immediately suggests this is not a one-off event.

The detailed description shows that the luxury is to be admired.

The visual description of the sumptuous feast tells the reader how in awe of the decadent scene the writer is.

When giving a response on comparing structure, you could:

* give an overview – present similarities between the source structures
* make clear links between the structure and the effect on the reader
* use direct quotations
* consider links between the opening and the rest of the text.

21st

Extract from Text 2, travel writing: lines 1–9 of the full text extract on page 174.

'Accès Interdit,' says the sign on the Quai des Milliardaires in Antibes. Behind a barrier the superyachts rise like a skyline in white and royal blue. This is the smartest address in a smart town. Riff-raff are discouraged.

Still, nobody pays much attention as I wander up to the first of these beasts, the motor yacht Katara. It is thought to have cost around $300m. You don't spend that much on a boat not to have anyone notice. Crew in white shirts and khaki shorts swarm over its decks, making final preparations to the scene. Everything is immaculate. Glasses and cutlery are laid on tables. Sun-loungers are set out on the teak transom, towels rolled in tight cylinders. On the top deck a helicopter waits. It all gleams in the sunshine.

The opening reference to the sign signals to the reader that access is restricted.

The detail of the opulence is portrayed in short, precise sentences and description.

Reinforces the idea of perfection.

Now try this

Give **three** examples of features of structure that you could compare.

Comparing language

Comparing how writers use language to express ideas can be challenging. You will need to do this in Paper 2.

Comparing language

When comparing the use of language in two source texts:

✓ **do** make direct comparisons between language features and their effects

✗ **don't** just write about the language in one text and then the language in the other text.

Extract from Text 1, The Great Gatsby: *lines 1–6 of the full text extract on page 173.*

There was music from my neighbor's house through the summer nights. On week-ends his Rolls-Royce became an omnibus, bearing parties to and from the city, between nine in the morning and long past midnight, while his station wagon scampered like a brisk yellow bug to meet all trains. And on Mondays eight servants including an extra gardener toiled all day with mops and scrubbing-brushes and hammers and garden-shears, repairing the ravages of the night before.

Extract from Text 2, travel writing: lines 19–23 of the full text extract on page 174.

Culinary choices are only the start of the potential tensions on board. Compared with the five-star hotel standard of the guest state-rooms, the crew accommodation is usually cramped and shared. Crew will wake up to serve breakfast and then stay until the last guest has gone to bed, meaning days can be up to 20 hours. There are no weekends at sea. On superyachts the owner is God, followed quickly by the captain and the guests.

---

1 You can either compare similar language features in the two texts and explore their effects...

Both sources are describing the lives of the wealthy from the perspective of onlookers. Both writers choose to describe these perspectives using references to time. For example, in Text 1, the writer describes the weekend party and Monday clear-up, and in Text 2, the writer describes the working pattern of the crew.

2 ... or you can compare similar effects created by different language techniques.

The perspective of the onlooker in Text 1 is one of excitement. Figurative language such as the 'station wagon scampered like a brisk yellow bug' glosses over the mundane task of what someone is doing – driving backwards and forwards to the station.

Text 2 uses straightforward descriptions of events: 'Crew will wake up to serve breakfast and then stay until the last guest has gone to bed, meaning days can be up to 20 hours'.

Now try this

Think about aspects of writers' language choices that you could compare. Give **three** examples.

Evaluating a text

Paper 1 will have a question that tests your ability to **evaluate** texts. Remember, 'evaluate' does not mean you comment about what you like or dislike about a text – an evaluation is not a review.

Approaching evaluation

A useful way to think about evaluation is to look at **how well** something is achieved rather than simply how it is achieved. For example, if you are asked about how successfully a writer creates tension, you do not need to look in detail at the connotations of individual words and techniques. Instead, you need to look at the specified text extract as a whole and discuss how well the writer has created tension overall.

> **Evaluate** (*verb*) To assess something and form an idea about its value.
>
> *Synonyms:* form an opinion of, make up one's mind about, analyse.

How to start an evaluation question

1
Read the question.
The question will tell you what aspect of the text to evaluate.

2
Read the text.
Look only at the specific lines or extract given in the question.

3
Annotate key quotations.
Plan and write your answer.

Look at pages 59–62 and 71–74 for more information on answering exam questions that ask you to evaluate.

Reading the text

Look at the **ideas**, **events**, **opinions**, **themes**, **intentions** and/or **viewpoints** of the text extract. Consider

- what happens or is described
- what the writer thinks or believes
- the tone of the text
- what the writer's purpose or intention is.

Think about how and why the writer uses these to create effects.

✓ Identify any key ideas, events, opinions, themes and intentions that relate to the question.

✓ Use inference to explain and assess (evaluate) the effects.

✓ Make a judgement – how well has the focus been achieved?

Explain your ideas in detail and support them with evidence.

Now try this

Read Text 1 on page 169 and identify one point you could make to answer this evaluation question:
In lines 9–15 the writer tries to demonstrate that visitors are impressed by the Great Exhibition.
Evaluate how successfully this is achieved.

Using evidence

In Papers 1 and 2, you need to use carefully selected and relevant evidence to support the points you make in your answers. Quotations can be long or short, but you must use them correctly in your answer to obtain maximum marks.

Using longer quotations

1 Introduce longer quotations with a colon.

2 Start the quotation on a new line.

3 Put your quotation in quotation marks.

4 Copy your quotation accurately.

5 Start your explanation on a new line.

Don't waste time writing out long quotations – consider paraphrasing or using a shorter quotation.

The writer uses alliteration and a personal pronoun in his opening paragraph:

'To add insult to injury, you then have to go to school.'

This helps to engage readers by creating a sarcastic tone that mocks modern teenagers, and sets out the writer's view that they are lazy.

P–E–E: Note how this answer correctly makes a point, supports it with evidence (the quotation), and then explains the effect.

The writer uses negative adjectives such as 'sullen' and 'resentful' to describe the way mothers feel that their teenagers behave. These words emphasise the lack of understanding that exists between parents and teenagers as they exaggerate the negative aspects of teenage behaviour.

Embedding quotations means that you can use more than one quotation in a sentence to fully evidence your points.

Using shorter quotations

1 You do not need to introduce each quotation with a colon or start a new line.

2 Put each quotation into quotation marks.

3 Make sure the sentence containing the embedded quotation makes sense.

4 Choose single-word quotations carefully to ensure you can make an effective comment on them.

Shorter quotations can be more effective than longer ones. They allow you to:

• identify key words and phrases

• focus on the writer's specific language choices.

Paraphrasing

Paraphrasing is referring closely to the text by turning it into your own words. Make sure your paraphrasing is closely linked to your understanding of the text, and clearly shows why you have chosen to paraphrase that section of text. Paraphrase:

• when the text you want to quote is long

• to avoid using too many quotations, which may weaken your answer

• for effective summaries.

Remember: paraphrasing is effective when evaluating the whole text, but use short quotations when you answer questions on language or structural techniques.

Now try this

Answer this question using both quotations and paraphrasing to present your evidence.

Look in detail at lines 1–14 of *The Great Gatsby* on page 173.

How does the writer use language to show the passage of time?

Writing questions: an overview

Both Paper 1 and Paper 2 of GCSE English Language 2.0 include a Writing section (Section B). There are different types of writing task in each paper.

Paper 1: Section B – Writing

Transactional writing

Write one response out of a choice of two tasks.

> Paper **1** tests your ability to write for different audiences and purposes, such as a letter or speech.

For more detailed information on Paper 1 Writing questions, see pages 29–36.

> It is possible that both writing question options in Paper 1 will ask you to write in the same form, for example a speech. If this happens, then the audience and/or purpose of the two options will be different.

Paper 2: Section B – Writing

Imaginative writing

Answer one question from a choice of two.

> Paper **2** tests your ability to write imaginatively.

For more detailed information on Paper 2 Writing questions, see pages 37–43.

Assessment objectives

Assessment objectives are the skills you are tested on in the exam questions. For Writing, the assessment objectives are the same for both papers.

> Remember what writing skills you will be tested on. The exam papers will not remind you.

Assessment Objective 5 tests your ability to:

* select the right tone for your writing and use the most appropriate language for your audience and purpose
* use sentences, paragraphs and grammar to organise and structure your writing so that the meaning is clear.

Assessment Objective 6 tests your ability to:

* use a range of vocabulary and sentence structures for clear and effective writing for the audience
* use accurate spelling and punctuation.

On **both papers**, look out for a note like this:

Your response will be marked for the accurate and appropriate use of vocabulary, spelling, punctuation and grammar.

You need to:

* vary the length and types of sentence you use
* spell and punctuate correctly
* use interesting and effective words.

Make sure you leave time to proofread your work when you have finished writing.

Refer to page 56 for information on proofreading.

Now try this

1 What kinds of writing do you need to do in Paper 1 and Paper 2?
2 How many writing questions do you need to answer for each paper?
3 Which paper or papers will require you to vary the length and type of your sentences?

Writing for a purpose: transactional

Paper 1: Section B – Writing will test the quality of your transactional writing skills. You need to show you can write effectively for different audiences and purposes.

What is transactional writing?

This type of writing is usually formal and includes:

- letters or formal emails
- speeches
- articles or reports
- reviews or blogs.

Within these forms you may be asked to write to:

- explain
- describe
- instruct/inform
- narrate.
- argue

> **Transactional writing** (noun) Writing to get things done; to inform or persuade a particular audience to understand or do something.

> Transactional writing is generally factual. Avoid using too much figurative language or rhetorical devices – use these when trying to persuade.

Purpose

The purpose of your writing will be to write in a particular form for a particular audience. This will be clear in the question, for example:

> Write a speech for 16-year-old students with the title 'How regular exercise can improve your learning'.

Form – the question will tell you explicitly what form to write in. Speeches need to inform, argue and persuade, and maintain a consistent point of view.

Audience – the audience you should write for will be clear in the question.

Topic – here the topic is exercise and learning.

> Section B will offer you a choice of two writing tasks. The forms they ask you to write in could be the same or different. If you have a choice of forms, consider which you can write most successfully in.

Tone

Choose your language and structure carefully to appeal to your audience. You might use formal, complex language for adults, or punchy, informal language for young people.

> A formal tone suggests to the reader that the information is professional and reliable.

Setting the right tone is vital. Think whether your writing is to be informal or instructive (formal). It is important to maintain a consistent tone throughout your piece of writing.

> Use Standard English – avoid informal language and slang.

Now try this

Identify the purpose, audience, form and tone for this sample question:
Write a letter of application to a local supermarket applying for a part-time job.

Ideas and planning: transactional

Planning will help you to structure your transactional writing for Paper 1: Section B. Taking time to plan your response is vital to produce a well-structured piece of writing, filled with relevant ideas and effective language.

Planning your transactional writing

> Write a speech for a school assembly with the title 'Video gaming is a harmful activity'.
>
> **(40 marks)**

See pages 79–82 for more information on understanding and answering Section B and the choice of question you will have.

You can write a balanced view or choose to focus on one side of the debate.

Plan: Harmless fun or an addiction?

Intro
The majority of teenagers play some form of video game on mobile or gaming devices – 60% of girls and 88% of boys

Plan your introduction to inform your audience of the topic and present your argument.

Add evidence to support key points.

Video games are violent
Opposing viewpoint: video games can be educational and are useful for learning.

Plan the key points by noting down the different ideas you can think of that support your viewpoint.

Addiction
Playing releases dopamine into the body, creating a feeling of pleasure.

Evidence: video games are made to be addictive.

Add opposing reasons and viewpoints and then follow up with why you agree or disagree that video gaming is harmful.

Limits social interaction
Video games fill the void for those who find it difficult to make real-world friendships, but it's no replacement for face-to-face interaction and practising social skills.

Opposing viewpoint: you can play with friends online, keep communicating and be part of a team.

Cyberbullying and online safety
Another way for someone to be bullied and potential exposure to online predators.

- Choose the most persuasive points and put those first.
- Don't be afraid to cross out some ideas that are weak or unnecessary.

Limits physical activity
Opposing viewpoint: ~~Always seated~~. Some interactive games can be a form of exercise as you need to walk outside to collect items in treasure hunt themed games.

Keep writing ideas!

Helps to develop life skills
In many games you need to work as part of a team, delegate and prioritise tasks.

You might want to change the order of your paragraphs once you have written your plan.

Develops problem-solving skills, which are useful for life.

Conclusion
Video games don't replace people or real-world experience. They can be a fun way to relax and socialise. Too much of one thing is never a good thing!

Plan a conclusion – your final point to round up.

Keep on referring back to the question as you plan. This will help to ensure that all of your points are relevant to the question.

Now try this

Write a plan for a speech for a school assembly with the title 'Television is **not** a waste of time'.

Writing for impact: transactional

In Paper 1 Section B – Writing, you will need to show you can write effectively for different transactional purposes. This may include writing that informs, explains or argues.

Argue and persuade

How effectively you present your point of view is based on the intensity of the key points you make in your writing.

To present your argument, focus on key points that highlight:

- why you are right
- why others, who may disagree, are wrong.

To persuade the reader:

- focus on what is wrong or at fault with the current situation
- suggest how your ideas will improve the situation.

Counter-arguments

When stating your opinion, consider the perspective of others who may disagree with you. Highlight why they are wrong and use adverbials to show you are rejecting that viewpoint.

Organising your writing

To help make your points effectively, break down your argument for the reader by starting a new paragraph for each new point you make.

In each paragraph you should:

- begin with a topic sentence – a sentence that clearly introduces the main point of the paragraph or links back to the previous paragraph
- develop the main point by explaining it in more detail and making any related points
- support your point with evidence, if appropriate.

See page 45 for ideas on how to link paragraphs and sentences with adverbial phrases.

Structure

Information and explanation texts:

- are usually organised chronologically (in the order of the events or in time order)
- use time phrases or temporal adverbials to provide signposts, for example:

In the morning... /First... /Then... /Next... /Finally...

The importance of evidence

It is vital that each key point you make is supported with evidence. This should be convincing. Include:

- quotations to support views
- statistics and facts
- expert comment and opinion
- personal experience.

Facts and statistics

Facts and statistics add authority to your writing. They provide convincing information and credible support to your response. If this information is not available from the sources provided, you can create your own – but make sure they are believable!

Rhetorical devices

Writers use these devices to emphasise their points or to manipulate the reader's response. They add power to your writing and engage the reader. Here are some rhetorical devices:

- rhetorical questions
- alliteration
- contrast
- pattern of three
- emotive language
- hyperbole
- direct address
- repetition
- lists

Now try this

Write a plan for an article for the school website with the title 'Parents – how you can help your child prepare for exams'.

Openings: transactional

How you start your writing and each paragraph is important to engage the reader and keep their interest throughout. There are different techniques you can use to effectively draw the reader in.

Effective openings

The first words need to immediately engage the reader and make them want to read more.

You can do this by using:

- **a bold statement**

> Recycling is a waste of time.

- **a quotation**

> 'Save our planet!' This chant was heard frequently at the recent demonstration in London.

- **a statistic or fact**

> 50% of all plastics ever manufactured have been made in the last 15 years.

> If the fact is surprising or the statistic is shocking this will also add impact, but be realistic.

- **a rhetorical question**

> Do we really want to stop climate change?

- **an interesting anecdote**

> At age four, I realised pollution was a problem when I found an oil-drenched bird on the beach.

> Remember to keep any anecdotes short and to the point.

> Don't tell the reader what you are going to do – just write it!
> ✗ In this article I am going to explain why recycling is important.
> ✓ Recycling takes minimal effort and is the least we can do to help stop climate change.

Continuing your topic

Once you have engaged the reader, you need to expand the point you want to make.

> The average person uses 100 kg of plastic each year. Are they doing all they can to limit their plastic usage? Or is plastic consumption so ingrained in our lives that they don't even notice what they are using?

A shocking statistic grabs the reader's attention. Here it makes them think about the volume of plastics they use.

Now try this

Read this question:

> Write an article for your school website with the title 'There is more to playing sport than winning'.

Write **three** possible opening sentences that would engage your readers' attention from the start.

Conclusions: transactional

In your Paper 1 Section B task, write an effective and memorable final paragraph to leave readers with a lasting impression. It is useful to include your conclusion in your planning.

Summing up

Plan your conclusion before you start writing. The final paragraph or conclusion to a text can be used to sum up your ideas – but avoid repeating them here. Equally, avoid adding new ideas in your conclusion. Instead, aim to sum up and emphasise your central idea. You could use one or more of these things.

End on a vivid image:	End on a warning:	End on a happy note:
a picture that lingers in the reader's mind.	what will happen if your ideas are not acted on?	emphasise how great things will be if your ideas are acted on.
A homeless person sits cold and alone in a shop doorway. As you pass by, you look into her eyes. She can't be older than 15.	Within 50 years, the world will have changed beyond all recognition – and our children will blame us for what has happened.	Ours could be the generation that made the difference.
End on a thought-provoking question:	**Refer back to your introduction:**	**End on a call to action:**
leave the reader thinking.	but don't repeat it.	make it clear what you want the reader to do.
For how long can we ignore what is staring us in the face?	I still have that dog – and he's still incredibly badly behaved. But if I hadn't…	Don't just sit there. Get up, get out and make it happen.

Remember that questions engage the reader with the issue – they will make them think how the subject relates to their own life.

Read through your writing and conclude it neatly. Leave your reader with a clear message.

Now try this

Read the example conclusions below and decide which type of summing up the writers have used.

1 The months of revision and exam preparation feel endless. But it will all be worth it!

2 We must all act now to stop the damage we are causing with our wastefulness. Now! Tomorrow is too late.

3 A dirty and dishevelled woman sits on the pavement, cold, alone and begging passers-by for money. Make the right choices now.

4 End pollution in our waterways now. Would you like to live amongst waste and debris?

5 If we don't invest in our health service now, we will pay the price in the years to come.

Form: articles and reviews

In Paper 1: Section B – Writing, you may be asked to write a newspaper or magazine article, or a review. You need to use the key features of the form you are being asked to write in.

Articles

Heading – this should provide clear information on the topic. Here it uses a rhetorical question, but it may use a pun, alliteration, repetition or other device to engage the reader.

Short opening sentence – this introduces the subject and summarises the key points. Later sentences add more detail.

Statistics – statistics from experts support the writer's point and make the article seem factual and reliable.

Quotations – Note the use of the correct punctuation.

> **Quotations and statistics**
>
> The quotations or evidence you use in your writing in the exam don't have to be real – but they must be believable and relevant, and use a tone and style appropriate to the audience you are writing for.

> **UNHAPPY AT WORK? IT'S TIME TO JOIN 'THE GREAT RESIGNATION'**
>
> It has been dubbed 'The Great Resignation'. British workers are planning to leave their jobs in droves. Recruitment firm Randstad UK surveyed 6,000 workers and found that 69 per cent of them would be happy to change jobs in the next few months. Nearly a quarter (24 per cent) were planning to move into a new role within three to six months.

> In the exam, you do not need to format your heading in bold capital letters. Your normal handwriting will do, with clear separation of the heading and body (content) of the article.

> Note that you may not always need to give a heading when writing an article. For example, the opening lines will be given to you in Question 7.

Reviews

Title of review – usually catchy to engage the reader and indicate the reviewer's opinion.

Engaging opening paragraph – often uses figurative language to give the reader a taste of what the film or event is like.

> Note that this structure and organisation is suitable for any type of review. This is for a film, but in the exam you may be asked to review a product, book, event or place.

> *Dune* review: **Masterful sci-fi adaptation is a classic Hollywood epic**
>
> As malicious forces burst into conflict over the planet's only supply of the most valuable resource in existence, Atreides, a gifted young man, must travel to the most dangerous planet in the universe. His mission? To ensure the future of his family and his people. Only those who can overcome their own fear will survive.
>
> Denis Villeneuve's *Dune* occasionally struggles with its unwieldy source material, but those issues are largely outshone by the extent and ambition of this visually electrifying adaptation. Once the slow-building story gets you hooked, you'll be on the edge of your seat and waiting for the sequel.

> **Now try this**
>
> Look at the article and the review on this page. List **three** differences in the features of these two forms.

Form: letters and reports

Knowing how to write letters and reports is a vital life skill that will help you beyond your GCSE English Language 2.0 exam.

Letters

Learn how to open and close your letter correctly.

- Use 'Dear Sir', 'Dear Madam' or 'To whom it may concern' if you do not know the name of the person you are writing to.

- End the letter with **Yours faithfully** if you use Dear Sir/Madam or To whom it may concern.

- End the letter with **Yours sincerely** if you use a name, for example Dear Ms Smith.

> Dear Madam
> I should be grateful if you would... .
> Yours faithfully
> Daniel Wallace

> Dear Ms Smith
> I am writing in response to the council's recent decision...
> Yours sincerely
> Esta Willis

Although the correct opening and closing lines are important, the most important thing is your writing in the body of the letter.

You should always ensure that the tone and content of your letter are appropriate to the person/people you are communicating with. Maintain the same tone throughout your letter.

Reports

Title – formal and factual.

Introduction – main facts about the topic.

Current situation – what is happening now.

Recommendation – an idea about what should change.

Conclusion – summarises the advantages of the proposed change.

The main purpose of reports is to inform and explain. They should be factual and formal and conclude with recommendations.

You can support these with your own opinions and viewpoints. All content should be relevant to the purpose of the report.

School marathon events

Most major cities across the world hold marathon events. These events collect thousands of pounds in sponsorship for charities, from the large, well-known national organisations to small, local ones that are personal to the runners.

Our school currently takes part in national events such as Comic Relief and Children in Need. Such events provide the school with an effective vehicle for teaching a variety of subjects in a way that engages students of all ages.

However, whilst they are well supported within the school they do not involve the wider community.

A school marathon would create an ideal opportunity to reach out...

So a sponsored school marathon event would combine two factors that are essential to a well-rounded education: physical activity and the promotion of empathy.

Now try this

Look at the letters and report on this page. Which form would be most suitable for the following tasks?

1 A request for a work experience placement with a local solicitor.
2 A proposal to create additional sports facilities in your town.
3 A thank you note to your elderly neighbour for the gift they sent you for your birthday.

Form: speeches, emails and blogs

In Paper 1 you may be asked to write a speech, formal email or blog post.

Speech writing

The most effective speeches argue an opinion or fact and aim to persuade the audience.

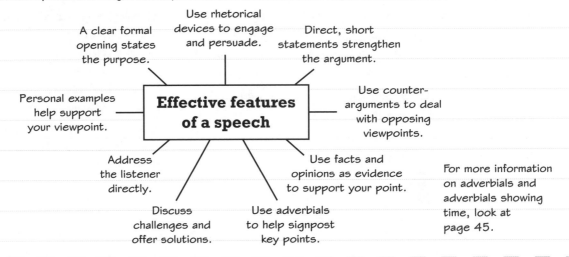

A clear formal opening states the purpose.

Use rhetorical devices to engage and persuade.

Direct, short statements strengthen the argument.

Personal examples help support your viewpoint.

Effective features of a speech

Use counter-arguments to deal with opposing viewpoints.

Address the listener directly.

Use facts and opinions as evidence to support your point.

For more information on adverbials and adverbials showing time, look at page 45.

Discuss challenges and offer solutions.

Use adverbials to help signpost key points.

Blogs

Blog is an abbreviation for 'web-log' – an online diary. Blogs can be written by anyone on any topic and take the form of diaries, reviews, recipe pages, etc. They are used both to inform and entertain and, as such, they often use informal language and are written in the first person. Additionally, they may not have a defined audience, other than someone interested in the subject matter. They may also include some of the following features:

- images and/or video clips
- varying fonts and text size
- weblinks.

Businesses and organisations often use blogs as informal communication to inform and engage their audience. Blogs can respond quickly to news and events, and can be updated easily.

To read about writing letters, go to page 34.

Formal emails

Email is now the most common form of business communication and is widely used in personal communications too – both with friends and family but also business contacts. Though emails are not generally as formal as letters, they still need to look and sound professional to present yourself and the subject of your communication clearly.

Now try this

Match the techniques (1–5) to the examples (A–E) provided.

1. Use rhetorical devices to engage and persuade
2. Use facts and opinions as evidence to support your point
3. Direct, short statements strengthen the argument
4. Personal examples help support your viewpoint
5. Use counter-arguments to deal with opposing viewpoints

A. Earlier today, I spoke with a young adult who was bullied via social media.
B. Of course meat is a source of protein, but we can find protein in other foods.
C. An overwhelming 97% of scientists agree that climate change is caused by human greenhouse gas emissions.
D. How can you sleep at night knowing this issue exists?
E. Think of our children. Think of our planet. Now is the time to act.

Vocabulary for effect: transactional

The vocabulary you select can have an important impact on your writing. In Paper 1 you will be asked to present a viewpoint that may require you to argue and persuade. Using a wide range of vocabulary including emotive words and positive and negative language will add impact to your writing.

Vocabulary for impact

Writers' word choices are made to encourage an emotional response in the reader. Using emotive language adds impact to your viewpoint or argument. For example, you may think that fast fashion is a problem. To prompt your reader to act, you want to highlight the issue by choosing emotive words. For example:

Fast fashion is a big problem.
Instead of 'big' consider: *immense, huge, mammoth*
Instead of 'problem' consider: *disaster, catastrophe, calamity*

Positive and negative language

If you structure your ideas using **positive** or **negative** language you can help guide and control the reader's reaction to your viewpoint. For example:

If you **support** teen use of social media, it could be described as: 'a vital network of support for isolated teens'.

If you **oppose** teens using social media, it could be described as: 'a network that encourages bullying and impacts on teen self-esteem'.

Connotations

You can guide your reader's reaction by thinking about the connotations of vocabulary. For example, look at the choices for completing this sentence, and what their connotations are:

Killing animals for food is...

brutal. ———emphasises violence.
barbaric. ———suggests uncivilised.
heartless. ———emphasises lack of feeling.

Rhetorical questions

Rhetorical questions are questions that can only really have one answer – the answer the writer wants! For example, 'Would you stand by and watch if you saw someone being bullied in this way?'

Using rhetorical questions is a useful tool to guide and persuade your audience.

They can also be used in creative writing to engage your reader. For example, 'What should I do?'

To learn more about rhetorical devices, see pages 30, 31 and 47.

Now try this

Rewrite the sentences below using emotive language to add impact.
1 Fox-hunting is cruel.
2 Plastic takes a long time to break down.
3 The minimum wage is too low.

Ideas and planning: imaginative

For Paper 2: Section B – Writing, you will need to write an imaginative response. It is important that you plan to allow yourself time to write a well-structured and developed answer.

The options

In the Paper 2 exam, you will be presented with two options for the writing task. For example:

> **EITHER**
>
> 7   Write an imaginative piece that starts with the line: 'I knew the minute I saw them that they were in danger'.
>
> **OR**
>
> 8   Write about a time when you, or someone you know, helped someone. Your response could be real or imagined. You may wish to base your response on one of the images or use any ideas of your own.
>
>

Planning

You can use different methods to plan – notes, tables, bullet points, spider diagrams – to keep your ideas focused on the main question. See which works best for you.

Ideas – picture it!

Take some time to picture the setting or the event – or look at the images provided if you choose Question 8. Consider what you can see:

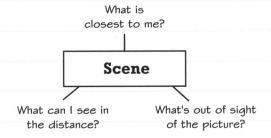

What is closest to me?

Scene

What can I see in the distance?   What's out of sight of the picture?

Ideas – characters and action

Now, consider the key characters and events.

Characters

- Who is there? Who are they?
- What are they like?
- How are they feeling? Why?
- How are they connected?

Events and action

- What is happening?
- What has happened?
- What will happen next?
- What are the characters doing?

Preparing the plan

✓ Choose the question you are going to answer. Which option gives you more ideas?

✓ Focus on a key event relating to the question topic.

✓ Consider which narrative voice to use. Use the first person (I/me) if you are the central character; third person (he/she) if it is from another perspective. (Note that you'll need to follow the line given if you choose Question 7.)

✓ Think about ideas for imaginative writing techniques.

✓ Plan ideas for four or five paragraphs. Spend around five minutes planning your response.

Now try this

Choose one of the Paper 2 exam-style questions above. Write down your initial ideas as either a list or a spider diagram.

Writing for an audience

In Section B of both papers, you will be assessed on your ability to communicate clearly, effectively and imaginatively showing that you can use the correct tone (the attitude of your writing) and style for different purposes and audiences. You will need to organise information and ideas using structural and grammatical features to support your ideas.

Writing for an adult audience

When writing for an adult audience, it is usually most appropriate to write using formal, Standard English language.

You should avoid using:

- colloquial language (e.g. The film was *ace*.)
- slang (e.g. It was *dope*.)
- double negatives (e.g. I *didn't do nothing*).
- abbreviated language (e.g. *IDK*).

Writing for a younger audience

For a younger or teenage audience, you should still avoid non-standard English, including slang and abbreviated language. However, to engage your audience it may be appropriate to use some informal language.

> Remember: in Section B of Paper 1 and Paper 2, your response will be marked for the accurate and appropriate use of vocabulary, spelling, punctuation and grammar.

Identifying the audience

In some questions, the person or people (**audience**) you are writing for may be clearly **stated**:

> 7   Write a speech for 14-year-old students with the title 'The benefits of sport and exercise'.   **(40 marks)**

Here, you know the age of your audience. Your writing must address and engage this age group. You could use carefully selected informal and figurative language to attract their attention.

> 8   Write a blog with the title 'Meat-free days – how making small changes to our diet can have a big impact'.
>
>   **(40 marks)**

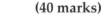

For this question, it is not stated who the audience is – or where the blog is posted. Think carefully about who would read it. Here, it would be advisable to assume a wide age range and plan your structure, writing and language carefully.

Also consider that blogs are generally more informal, opinion articles.

Now try this

1   Describe the implied audience for this question:
    Write an article for a broadsheet newspaper with the title 'Video games are too violent for our children'.

2   Read the following sentence written in response to question 1. Does it have the appropriate tone and language for the audience? Rewrite it to improve it.

> No way! It's not real. I've never heard no one do anything stupid after playing a game.

Writing for a purpose: imaginative

Before writing your imaginative piece for Paper 2: Section B, think about the form and structure.

Form

Writers produce text in different forms, such as a short story, novel or memoir. In the Paper 2 exam, you could write a narrative, monologue or descriptive piece. Understanding the difference between the forms will help you make the right choice for your own piece of writing.

- **Narrative** – a story that you have made up. It should have a beginning, progress through a series of scenes of action, and have an ending.

- **Descriptive** – a piece that describes something: an event, a place or another person. It could be real or made up. It should be vivid and detailed, so the reader can imagine the subject.

- **Monologue** – a long speech given by one person. The person could be yourself or someone else, real or imagined. The whole story or description is told from their point of view.

Structure

Unless the question specifically says otherwise, your writing should have a clear:

- beginning   • middle   • end.

1 **Beginning** – set the scene. Don't rush to provide all the information in your opening paragraph. Hints at what is to come will keep the reader engaged.

2 **Middle** – in a story, this is where the action often happens or where something happens to the character(s). In a descriptive piece, it's where your description really begins to paint a picture.

3 **End** – when you plan your writing you need to decide how it ends.

   a A story needs to have an ending that makes sense and satisfies the reader. Endings can be happy or sad, or even end on a cliffhanger, as long as it fits with what you have already written.

   b For descriptive pieces and monologues, try to come to a conclusion that leaves the reader feeling satisfied. For example, if you are writing about an event, try to write about what happened at the end of the night/day.

TOP TIP

All good characters have a goal – and all good stories have a conflict that prevents them from getting what they want.

Question 7 in Paper 2 will give you an opening sentence. You will need to continue your beginning logically from that sentence.

Do

✓ focus on key dramatic elements

✓ focus on important events

✓ focus on simplicity.

Don't

✗ overload on plot detail and action

✗ write about events that are not relevant

✗ have too many characters, settings, events – there won't be time to develop them all.

Now try this

1 Suggest ways that these ideas could be 'shown' rather than 'told'.

   a It was a cold day.   **b** She was happy.   **c** They were tired.   **d** He was frightened.

2 Using the idea of a hot day, write an imaginative example for each figurative language device.

   a Simile   **b** Metaphor   **c** Personification

Writing for impact: imaginative

The focus of Paper 2: Section B – Writing is imaginative writing. There are several techniques you can use to help engage the reader and develop your response.

The five senses

The five senses are:

- sight
- sound
- touch.
- smell
- taste

Using senses in your description helps the reader to picture the scene.

> The metallic taste of blood roused me before I felt the warm trickle down my cheek. There was nothing before me, only black. The droning of the cars somewhere distant gave me no clue as to where I was.

Use of the senses of touch ('felt') and sound ('droning') makes the description vivid and engages the reader.

Try to **show**, not **tell**. A paragraph starting 'he saw', followed by 'then he smelt' and 'later he touched' is unlikely to engage the reader.

> I laughed and felt at ease.

> A cheery chuckle came from within as I felt the anxiety flow away, and I stood up and confidently made my way to the stage.

Narrative voice and feelings

Unless you are given specific instructions in the exam paper, you can choose which narrative voice to use – **first** or **third person**. It is important that you maintain the same narrative voice throughout your writing. Where you are given an opening sentence in the first or third person, be sure to continue in the same way.

First person: I, me, my, mine, myself, we, our, ours, ourselves …

Third person: she, he, hers, his, they, theirs …

First person narration can help the reader connect with the narrator.

You can also describe the narrator's feelings as a way to enhance your writing. Showing the reader how the narrator feels is much more powerful than telling them.

— Here, the reader is told directly how the narrator feels.

— The adjective helps the reader imagine the narrator's physical reaction.

Figurative language

Used carefully, figurative language creates strong images in the reader's mind. However, it is important to use devices such as **metaphors**, **similes** and **personification** while still making sense. Similes like 'They fought like cats and dogs' and metaphors such as 'heart of stone' are not very imaginative.

Avoid using too many figurative devices or descriptive techniques.

This stronger verb gives the reader an immediate image.

Vocabulary choice

Choose your words carefully. Using fewer – but considered – words will be much more effective.

When describing, try not to use 'very', e.g. very big, very fast. Instead think of their synonyms, e.g. immense, hastily.

> I ran quickly across the field like I was a sprinter in a race.

> I raced across the field.

Now try this

Using strong verbs can help to improve your descriptive writing. Replace these phrases with single verbs.

| he spoke quietly | it ended suddenly | she walked slowly |

40

Structure: imaginative

In Paper 2: Section B – Writing you will need to structure your imaginative writing effectively. Using a narrative structure can help you plan and develop your response.

Narrative structure

In Paper 2, you may have to write a short story. Short stories work best when they are clearly constructed around a narrative structure like this example:

1 **Exposition:** the beginning.

Establish the setting and characters.

Think about using some of the five senses in your writing.

2 **Complication:** introducing the issue or conflict.

Introduce the main issue or conflict. Focus on engaging the reader by creating tension and excitement.

Use metaphors or similes.

3 **Crisis:** the climax.

Link to the main event, issue or conflict facing the characters. After this the story can start to wind down.

Use dramatic adjectives or verbs.

4 **Resolution:** the ending.

Resolve any issues so the reader is left with a clear understanding of what has happened and conclude on a happy or a sad note.

You could mix up the narrative structure. Start at the crisis and use flashbacks to the exposition and complication.

TOP TIP

Be careful not to spend too long on the exposition. As well as using this structure to plan your writing, you can use it to plan your time and think carefully how much time you will need for each section.

Now try this

Complete the narrative structure for this question: Write about a time when you, or someone you know, had to change plans. Your response could be real or imagined.

Include ideas about creative writing techniques in your plan.

Note down which narrative viewpoint you will use: first person or third person.

Beginnings and endings: imaginative

How you choose to open and conclude your piece of imaginative writing is very important. Both of these elements are crucial to engage and draw in your reader and create impact.

The beginning

Sometimes the beginning is referred to as the 'opening', 'exposition' or 'introduction'.

Use this part of your narrative structure to:

- instantly engage the reader
- set the tone for the rest of your writing.

Use features such as dialogue, danger, description or mystery to connect with the reader.

Description

Using a vivid description in your exposition helps to set the scene and allows the reader to visualise the setting and/or characters.

It also presents opportunities to use imaginative writing techniques.

Figurative language: simile and alliteration.

Bounding and swirling in the shadowy dusk, the unfurling flames flew effortlessly like dancers. Hypnotised by the dazzling sun in front of me, I just stood. The heat gripped me first. Then the noise. Then the fear.

Sentence structure: long followed by short sentences.

Dialogue

Opening your writing with speech conveys ideas about your character(s).

'Leave me alone!' Cheeks burning, eyes stinging, Tyler picked himself up off the ground.

Mystery

Playing around with your narrative structure and starting at the crisis and using flashbacks can be an engaging way to begin your writing.

I am trapped, frightened, alone.

Danger

Introducing drama and danger in your opening creates tension, drawing the reader in.

Something grabbed me, pulling me down. Gasping, choking I punched through the watery ceiling clutching for air.

The ending

The ending, or resolution, is important as it will leave the reader with a final impression of your writing.

- Plan the tone – amusing, sad or happy?
- Make sure the tone of the resolution fits with the rest of your writing – don't jump between happy and moving.
- Avoid ending with a cliché like 'it was all a dream'.
- Make your final sentence count. Think carefully about what you are saying and how you are saying it.

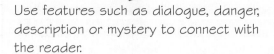

Now try this

There are different styles of opening that you can use in your imaginative writing. Write a beginning that sets a tone of fear or concern using each of the following styles:

- Dialogue
- Senses to set the scene
- Mystery
- Description of action

Vocabulary for effect: imaginative

The vocabulary you select can have an important impact on your writing. In Paper 2 you will be asked to write an imaginative response.

Choose your words carefully

The best descriptive and creative writing 'shows' the reader rather than 'tells' them. Carefully chosen verbs can be particularly effective.

> ✗ She walked decisively through the station.

> ✓ She marched through the station.

Equally, showing the reader sometimes takes more words than telling them. Two useful rules are:

Don't name your feelings.

> ✗ I felt really nervous.

> ✓ My heart raced, blood flushed my cheeks...

Do describe the effect they have on you.

> ✗ It burned me.

> ✓ The searing heat sent shockwaves through my hand.

Focus on what matters

You don't need to describe everything. For example, if you want to describe a scream in the night, keep to the relevant detail.

> ✓ The piercing screech jolted me awake. The darkness gave no clue to the source.

> ✗ The alarm of the yell woke me suddenly from my sleep. The darkness was all around me. I couldn't make out where the scream had come from.

Describing people

Focus on details that give the reader a vivid image of a person. Avoid generic details but concentrate on details that hint at character.

✗ Blonde hair   ✓ Scuffed shoes

✗ Black coat   ✓ Dirty fingernails

Don't use too many words

Sometimes less is more. If you use too many adjectives and adverbs it can reduce the impact.

> ✗ The moon's glowing, majestic, shimmering haze penetrated the room, throwing curtains of white light across the walls.

Synonyms

Synonyms are words that have similar meanings, and using them makes your writing more interesting. Using a range of synonyms for key words and ideas ensures that:

- you don't repeat the same key word throughout your writing
- you can pick the most precise word – the one that really says what you mean.

Now try this

Give at least two synonyms for each of these words:
- violent
- cloudy
- large
- stopped
- smiled

Paragraphs

Use paragraphs to structure and organise your written responses. Structuring your writing this way helps you to clearly present new information in transactional writing and new characters and themes within your imaginative response.

You will need to use paragraphs for your writing in both papers.

Paragraphs

Paragraphs break up your writing into clear sections. They help the reader to follow the information and make the text easier to read.

> Spend a few minutes planning the points you want to make. Each time you introduce a new point, start a new paragraph.
>
> one paragraph = one point

Paragraphing for effect

Generally, you should start a new paragraph when you start a new point.

However, shorter paragraphs are an effective way to create dramatic pauses, tension or pace within your writing. They also emphasise key points.

Structuring paragraphs: argue and persuade

Use Point–Evidence–Explain to structure paragraphs in a piece of writing to argue or persuade.

A short, clear point.

Evidence to support the point.

Explains how the point and evidence are relevant to the main idea.

> • Our global climate is changing.
> • Each year is declared the coldest, driest, hottest or wettest since records began.
> • It has clearly become a significant threat to our planet, and without immediate action we are heading for disaster. What does it take for the world to wake up to this issue?

Structuring paragraphs: inform, explain, review

Start each paragraph with a topic sentence – a sentence that clearly introduces the reader to the content of the paragraph. Use the remainder of the paragraph to develop and add detail to the topic sentence.

Topic sentence.

Detail/development.

> • Our community has made striding efforts to reduce food waste.
> • Every Wednesday The Free Fridge is open to everyone. It is stocked with food donated by supermarkets and shops which they would otherwise throw out.

> When writing to inform, explain or describe, start each paragraph with a topic sentence expressing the main idea of that paragraph.

Now try this

Write one paragraph in response to this sample question:

Write a report for your head of year with the title 'Improving provision of extra-curricular activities available in our school'.

Linking ideas with adverbials

Use adverbials to guide the reader through your ideas. They work to show the reader the direction that your ideas are taking.

Adding an idea

Moreover,...

Furthermore,...

In addition,...

Likewise,...

> Park closures at night will not address the problem. **Furthermore**, they could create issues elsewhere.

Explaining

As a result,...

Therefore,...

Consequently,...

> The town has inadequate facilities for teens and young adults. **Consequently**, the number of complaints about antisocial behaviour has increased.

Illustrating

For example,...

For instance,...

...such as...

> **For instance**, young people are often the first to be blamed for littering.

Emphasising

in particular

especially

significantly

chiefly

> There are many dog-walkers in town, **especially** in areas that are used by the wider community.

Comparing and contrasting

Comparing	Contrasting
Similarly	However
Likewise	On the other hand
In the same way	On the contrary

> It is claimed that grouse shooting is a valuable asset to the Scottish economy. **Likewise**, fox hunting supports lots of rural jobs. **However**, animal welfare campaigners say...

Showing time

Afterwards	At this moment	Before
Later	Meanwhile	Then
Previously	After a while	

> **Time** or **temporal** adverbials are useful ways to indicate the passing of time in imaginative writing.

> Just **at this moment**, in this place everything seemed perfect. The sun, the moon, the stars aligned. **Before** today I never thought it possible.

Now try this

Think of a topic that interests you (e.g. gaming, playing sport, healthy lifestyle). Write sentences about the topic using different adverbials for each purpose.

1 Comparing   2 Showing time   3 Adding an idea

4 Explaining   5 Emphasising   6 Illustrating

Language for different effects 1

Using different language techniques effectively adds impact to your writing. Developing these skills will be useful in both Paper 1 and Paper 2 responses.

Rhetorical questions

These are an effective way to hook the reader's interest and get them to consider their own point of view and response to the question.

As a persuasive tool they add impact to an argument and point of view. Use these in argument or persuasive writing to lead the reader to the answer you want.

'Are we a nation that accepts the cruelty of ripping children from their parents' arms? Or are we a nation that values families, and works to keep them together?'

Using them in creative writing engages the reader in the situation.

'If you prick us, do we not bleed? If you tickle us, do we not laugh?'

Contrast

When two opposing ideas are placed together, they provide a direct contrast and emphasise the difference.

You can work hard in a job you hate for the rest of your life...

or you can work hard on your education and give yourself the opportunity to get the job you want.

Using contrast in creative writing exaggerates detail.

The audience rose to their feet, clapping, cheering. Except one man. He sat, stony faced, glaring at the stage.

Remember that rhetorical questions will end with a question mark.

Repetition

Repeating words and phrases adds emphasis to key ideas within an argument.

Apples wrapped in plastic. Meat wrapped in plastic. Cheese wrapped in plastic, all carried in bags made of plastic.

The same tool can also emphasise ideas in creative writing.

Stay silent for one minute, be afraid for one minute, stay hidden for one minute. Then run.

Lists

Lists are a useful way to introduce a variety of ideas in your writing.

It's slow, tough, tiring and expensive.

In creative writing, lists add to descriptions.

Strewn across the field were bottles, cans, bags of rubbish, discarded tents.

Now try this

Look at the sentences below and say if the language technique used is:

   a contrast   **b** repetition   **c** rhetorical question   **d** list.

1 How could she do this?
2 Panic all around me. Commuters running, people screaming, police officers shouting.
3 There was only one answer. There was only one way out of this situation.
4 When the depths of darkness fall, no light will ever rise.
5 The dirt and debris of the day receded as blue, cleansing sea rolled up the shore.
6 How could she have believed this to be true?

Language for different effects 2

Language techniques can add power and impact to your writing. These techniques will mainly be useful for your transactional writing for Paper 1, but you could also use them in your imaginative writing for Paper 2.

Direct address

Talking directly to the reader can be very persuasive.

Using 'you' suggests that your ideas are relevant to them. For example:

> 'You understand the pressure of exams.'

Using 'we' creates a bond between the writer and the reader. It suggests commonality.

> 'If we don't face up to our responsibilities now, we won't have the chance again. It is up to us to initiate change.'

Pattern of three

Linking words or phrases in groups of three adds rhythm and emphasis to your ideas in all kinds of writing.

> The work involved blood, sweat and tears.

> Exercise benefits your head, your heart and your happiness.

> I stood up in front of the class, my face prickly, warm and pink.

Alliteration

Alliteration adds rhythm and emphasis to your writing. Remember: the alliterative words do not have to be next to each other – just near each other.

> It was an arduous adventure.

> Combined with other language techniques, alliteration can be particularly engaging and powerful: The frantic, flowing flames...

Hyperbole

> **Hyperbole** (noun) Exaggerated statements or claims not meant to be taken literally.

Exaggeration can add humour to both an argument and a description.

> It felt like I had walked for a million miles and a thousand years.

It can also emphasise a key point within your writing.

> Teachers want their students to sit completely still and in total silence for six hours a day.

Now try this

Rewrite each example sentence in three ways using:

    a direct address   **b** pattern of three   **c** alliteration.

1 Many people don't recycle.
2 Public speaking can be a daunting experience.

Starting a sentence

The way you start off your sentences can help add interest to your responses in both Paper 1 and Paper 2.

First words

The way in which you begin a sentence determines its tone. For example, an adverb will immediately suggest action:

> Silently, I crept towards the door.

A pronoun will focus the reader on a particular character or characters:

> She opened the door, snorted and then burst out laughing.

An adjective will draw the reader's attention to how something looks, feels, sounds, smells or tastes:

> Acrid smoke smothered my lungs.

Developing writers often start their sentences in similar ways. Try to start your sentences in different ways to engage your reader. You can start with any of these.

Type of word	Examples
A pronoun I, you, he, she, it, we, they, my, your	She watched and listened.
An article a, an, the	A rainbow appeared.
A preposition at, before, behind, below, with, etc.	Below me, I saw the busy streets.
An -ing word (or present participle) scowling, slowing, racing, frowning, etc.	Crawling slowly through the cavern, I made my way towards the light.
An adjective quick, thunderous, tiny, calm, etc.	Sticky, golden honey dripped down the spoon.
An adverb willingly, cheerfully, sadly, etc.	Warily, I opened the door.
A conjunction (subordinate clause + main clause) if, although, because, when, while, etc.	Although I knew I was in an empty house, I could not help thinking that I was not alone.

Now try this

Using each of the seven types of sentence opener above, write seven sentences about the most memorable moment of your childhood.

Sentences for different effects

How you structure your sentences can have different effects. For example, in your imaginative writing you can use sentence structure to achieve a particular tone or mood. In a piece of transactional writing, your structure can emphasise a point of view.

Longer sentences

By using long, multi-clause sentences, you can deliver more information concisely.

Use subordinate clauses to add information, such as in the example.

Don't confuse the reader with masses of information across lots of subordinate clauses.

The city, which I had never visited before, felt like home.

— Main clause
— Subordinate clause

Commas separate the two clauses.

Mixing it up – long and short

Short, single-clause sentences are effective as they add tension, suspense and surprise to a description, or impact to an argument.

Short, single-clause sentences are particularly effective when they follow a longer, multi-clause sentence.

I sauntered through the winding backstreets of Florence, soaking up the fading autumn sun and the reflective peace and quiet of age-old streets unburdened by tourists, turning left and right onto paths unknown. A traveller's paradise.

Short sentence contrasts with a long sentence to surprise the reader.

In order of importance

Important information is usually placed at the end of a sentence. You can control the structure of your sentences to provide the biggest impact.

Arrange your sentences so that the point you want to emphasise comes at the end.

This sentence places more emphasis on feeling nervous because that comes at the end of the sentence.

Even though I had revised and prepared for the dreaded exam, I still felt nervous.

This sentence emphasises the dreaded exam, giving the sentence more impact:

I still felt nervous even though I had revised and prepared for the dreaded exam.

Now try this

Write two or three sentences in response to the question.
Aim to include:
- a long sentence followed by a short sentence
- a sentence structured to leave the important information until the end.

Write a speech for an assembly with the title 'The importance of volunteering'.
You should include:
- how and where to volunteer and why it is a valuable experience
- how to overcome possible difficulties for volunteers
- the advantages of helping others.

Formal and informal language

It is vital that you write appropriately for your audience. As a rule, you should always use formal language (Standard English) unless writing to someone familiar to you when it would be appropriate to use more informal language.

Formal language

We often use formal language when we write. It is less personal but more respectful of an audience that you do not know.

The tone of your language – register – is also important to consider for the purpose and the audience. You need to determine the level of formality that is appropriate for your communication.

Consider your word choices and ensure you write clear sentences and use appropriate punctuation. This will help to convey your purpose such as 'persuade' or 'inform'.

When to use formal language

- Exams
- Essays and reports
- Business communications; job applications
- Presentations
- Letters and emails to people you don't know.

> I am writing to you, the Council Leader, to express my concern over the lack of funding for sporting facilities in our local area.

Here, the tone and language used are clear. It is to the point and respectful of the intended audience.

Informal language

Even when a question asks you to write to someone you know, your purpose should still be clearly understood.

Slang, most often used in speech, is the most informal language. It may not be clearly understood by everyone.

Colloquial language is functional and normally used in informal conversations. It is a form of slang and some terms or words may only be used by specific social groups or in particular regions of the country.

When to use informal language

- Conversations with friends
- Writing speech or conversations
- Personal emails and letters
- Social media posts and comments.

Colloquial

> Mate, you ain't gonna believe it but I only went and scored a screamer in the match.

Slang

Here, the tone and language used are clear too. The informality and use of slang are appropriate for the casual communication between friends.

Now try this

1 What is the correct language style (formal or informal) for each of the following purposes?

   a   A social media comment

   b   An email for a job application

   c   A journal entry

   d   A letter to your local MP

2 Rewrite the sentences below in formal language.

   a   If you have any questions, just shout!

   b   Sorry, I'm busy that day.

Commas

Using commas correctly is a very important feature of your writing. You can use them to separate extra information (subordinate clause) from the main part of the sentence (main clause). You can also use them to separate nouns, verbs and adjectives within lists.

Commas and subordinate clauses

When you use two clauses in a sentence and start with the main clause you **do not** need a comma to separate the clauses.

When you use two clauses in a sentence and you start with the subordinate clause, you **do** need a comma to separate the clauses.

> I cleaned my bedroom as it was messy.

Main clause starts the sentence.

> As it was messy, I cleaned my bedroom.

Subordinate clause starts the sentence and is followed by a comma.

Commas and relative clauses

When adding extra information to a sentence, you can link it with a relative pronoun such as that, who, when, which and where. This creates a relative clause.

The relative clause should always be separated from the main clause with a comma.

> The village, where children had always played in the past, is a quiet place.

Main clause.   Relative clause.

Note how commas separate the two clauses.

Commas in lists

When you are writing a list, use a comma after each word or phrase. Remember to use **and** or **or** before the final word or phrase.

> She ordered noodles, chicken, soup and orange juice.

No comma is needed here as **and** is used before the final item in the list.

> He was short, unkempt and unfashionable.

A comma is used here to separate two adjectives.

Now try this

1 Rewrite the sentence to include the additional information:

   Sentence: Florence has amazing museums and architecture.

   Additional information: the most beautiful city in the world

2 Correct the sentence by adding commas where they are needed.

   Tom's present list included computer games books chocolate football boots and a football.

Apostrophes and speech punctuation

Missing or incorrect apostrophes and speech punctuation are common mistakes. Make sure you know how to use both correctly to avoid errors.

Apostrophes in contractions

When two words are shortened (contracted or abbreviated), they make speech sound more informal and natural. In contracted words you should use an apostrophe to show where letters are missing.

You are → **You're**

We will → **We'll**

Let us → **Let's**

Think about your audience when you use abbreviations. The full version might be more appropriate in formal writing.

Apostrophes of possession

Apostrophes can be used to show that something belongs to something or someone else.

- The bird's song
- Arun's car
- The Prime Minister's speech.

When the word you are adding an apostrophe to already ends in 's' (such as in plural nouns), you add the apostrophe after the 's':

- The boys' mothers

When a name ends in 's' you add an apostrophe and then you can add another 's'. Both of these are correct:

Miles' dog   Miles's dog

Speech punctuation

You should always use speech marks to show when words are spoken. Speech marks are also known as quotation marks or inverted commas.

Other rules to follow in speech are:

- Start the speech with a capital letter.
- Use a punctuation mark before the closing speech mark.
- Always use a comma if you are saying who is speaking, with a lower-case letter after the closing speech mark.
- Use a full stop before the speech mark if you are not continuing by saying who is speaking.

'Enjoy what you do and you will never work a day in your life,' said Grandma wisely.

'Breakfast is ready,' shouted Dad.

'We need to be there for 8 p.m.'

Now try this

1 Write the contractions for the word pairs below.

I will   do not   would have   They are

2 Rewrite these sentences using contractions and correct punctuation.

a I would not like to go sky diving shivered Sam.

b The hockey sticks are not in the cupboard shouted Sohail. They are already on the field replied Mr Cook.

Colons, semicolons, brackets and dashes

Colons

Use a colon to introduce additional information or an explanation.

> There's just one problem with the egg: it's broken.

With a colon, you can clearly define the break between your words and a quotation.

> In *As You Like it*, Shakespeare presents the image of life as a play: "All the world's a stage…"

The colon helps to present a list of information clearly.

> For my holiday I need: a swimsuit, sun cream, a hat and a good book.

Semicolons

Use semicolons to separate items such as in a long list. If a list already contains commas, the semicolon avoids confusion between the items.

> We plan to visit Paris, France; Seville, Spain; and Lisbon, Portugal.

You can also use a semicolon in place of a conjunction.

> The concert sold out(;) I couldn't get a ticket. The concert sold out (and) I couldn't get a ticket.

Brackets

Brackets can be used when providing extra information. Use brackets in pairs, putting one bracket before the extra information and one after it.

> Owain (who hates running) signed up to run a marathon.

Note that you could use commas instead of brackets, but that would make the sentence a little more formal.

Dashes

Dashes can be used in pairs to introduce information in the middle of a sentence.

> My parents met – 26 years ago – when they worked in a hospital.

You can also use a single dash at the end of a sentence to introduce an afterthought or suggest a pause.

> We never did find my missing shoe – I think the dog ate it.

Now try this

1 Rewrite the sentence below including colons and any other punctuation needed.
  The rainbow contains seven colours red orange yellow green blue indigo and violet.

2 Which sentence has the correct punctuation?
  a Toby loves pizza; Sohail does not.   **b** Toby loves; pizza Sohail does not.

3 Rewrite the sentences below, adding the bracketed information in the correct places.
  a Shakespeare wrote over 150 sonnets. (who was also a prolific playwright)
  b Neil Armstrong got his pilot's licence before he learned to drive a car. (the first man on the moon)

4 Add dashes in the correct places in the sentences below.
  a Marcus Rashford who plays football for England led a campaign against child poverty.
  b The fair which began in 1652 is held each September.

Common spelling errors 1

Spelling is a vital part of writing. You will need to show you can spell correctly and avoid simple errors that can cost you marks in your exam papers.

Their, there, they're

These three words are often confused, but they all mean very different things.

- **Their** means belonging to them.
- **There** describes the position or location of something.
- **They're** is an abbreviation of 'they are'.

They're getting changed into **their** kits in the room over **there**.

Two, too, to

Two is the word for number 2.
E.g.: It is a **two**-bedroom house.

Too is used to show an addition or excessive amount.

E.g.: He wants to see the film **too**.
I ate **too** much pizza.

To is used to show movement towards a direction or place.
E.g.: I am going **to** the hospital.

Or **to** goes before a second verb.
E.g.: She went **to** see the animals.

Where, wear, were, we're

All of these words sound similar but again they mean very different things.

Where refers to a place and can be a question word.
E.g.: **Where** are you going? / We know **where** it is.

Wear is a verb related to clothes.
E.g.: I have nothing in my wardrobe to **wear**!

Were is the past tense of 'are'.
E.g.: The crowds **were** cheering.

We're is an abbreviation of 'we are'.
E.g.: **We're** going on holiday next week.

Test yourself by writing or explaining to someone when to use the words on this page.

Are, our

Another common error is confusion about how to use these two words.

Our means something belongs to us.
E.g.: **Our** dog barks all the time.

Are is the plural form of 'is'.
E.g.: My parents **are** moving to Scotland.

Would have, could have, should have

A common mistake is to write 'would of', 'should of' or 'could of', using 'of' in place of 'have'. Use of 'of' in these examples is grammatically incorrect.

E.g. Global warming **could have** been slowed down. We **should have** stopped burning fossil fuels long ago.

Now try this

Circle the correct word to use in each sentence.

Their / There / They're the best band in the world.

I would like to / two / too cappuccinos please.

We were / where / wear / we're going to travel for a year but Covid-19 meant we couldn't go.

Our / Are family tree can be traced back to the year 1365.

Common spelling errors 2

Learn how to avoid spelling errors.

Your, you're

These are two different words with different meanings:

- **your** means belonging to you
- **you're** is the abbreviation of **you are**.

> ✗ You're time starts when your ready.

> ✓ Your time starts when you're ready.

Off, of

These are two easily confused words but their sound is different:

- **off** rhymes with cough
- **of** is pronounced **ov**.

> ✗ The bird flew of the top branch off the tree.

> ✓ The bird flew off the top branch of the tree.

Its, it's

Using punctuation correctly is very important.

- **It's** is an abbreviation of **it is**.
- **Its** means belonging to **it**.

> ✗ Its the start of it's life.

> ✓ It's the start of its life.

Effect, affect

Understand word classes and use them correctly.

- **Effect** is normally used as a noun.
- **Affect** is a verb.

For example, you may have been **affected** by remote learning. But remote learning had an **effect** on you.

Whose, who's

- **Who's** is an abbreviation of 'who is' and can be a question word.
- **Whose** expresses belonging and can be a question word.

> ✗ Whose wearing who's boots?

> ✓ Who's wearing whose boots?

Passed, past

Try not to confuse these two words.

- Passed is the past tense of the verb 'to pass', e.g. **She passed her driving test.**
- Past refers to position or time, e.g. **They sprinted past the opposition. It's all in the past.**

Now try this

Find the eight errors in this piece of writing and correct them.

Your not going to believe what happened today. I was walking passed the bus stop when out off nowhere, a learner driver drove of the road. He crashed into a wall. Thankfully the driver was ok, but I am sure it will have an affect on him. Its frightening to think how easily accidents can happen. I don't know who's fault it was – if anyone's. I think a tyre burst. Either way, I don't think he will have past if he was taking his test.

Proofreading

It is vital to plan for time at the end of your exam to check your work and correct any mistakes.

Common mistakes

When writing under pressure and in a hurry, most people will make mistakes. The most frequent are:

* spelling errors
* incorrect or missing punctuation
* grammar errors such as missing words.

TOP TIP

If a word doesn't look right and you know it is spelt incorrectly, practise writing it different ways on note paper or in the margin. You might know the correct spelling when you see it.

Useful strategies

* Reading out loud is a good way to make sure that you have written what you wanted to write. Obviously, in an exam situation you can't do this, but you can read aloud in your head.
* Reading your work backwards focuses your attention on spelling rather than the meaning of your work.
* Check for one type of error at a time to focus your attention.

Making corrections

Make sure you make any corrections clearly so your changes are obvious to the reader.

* Use a single line through your mistake – a word or a sentence.
* To add a new word or sentence, use ∧ or *

I have made ∧ mistake.
^a

Always * ~~at the proofread end of your exam.~~
*proofread at the end of your exam.

If you have missed the start of a new paragraph, add // to show where the break between paragraphs should be.

Proofreading checklist

✓ Correct any spelling mistakes.

✓ Correct any missing or incorrect punctuation.

✓ Check for repeated or missing words.

✓ Look for sentences that are unclear or clumsy.

✓ Make sure your changes are clear.

✓ If you have time and have answered all your questions, proofread it again!

Now try this

Cross out and correct all the errors you can find in this text:

The Covid-19 pendamic had huge affect on everyone, but particularly young people. lockdowns and periods of elf-isolation meant that when they should of been experiencing life, the world outside of home was unavailable

Understanding Question 1

Question 1 will always be structured in the same way. Make sure you know how it works and what it is asking you to do.

How does Question 1 work?

Question 1 will always focus on Text 1.

In the exam, you will find source texts in the separate Source Booklet.

Question 1 will always ask you to find four different pieces of information.

1   Read <u>Text 1</u> in the <u>Source Booklet</u> provided. <u>Identify four items that were on display at the exhibition in the Crystal Palace.</u>

(4 marks)

Write your answers in the <u>space provided</u>.

This is the topic of the question. Read the question carefully to make sure you know what information you need to find.

Write one answer in each of the spaces. Try not to write too much – one phrase or sentence for each point will be enough.

Check how many marks this question is worth. This will help you to manage your time.

What does Question 1 assess?

✓ Question 1 tests Assessment Objective 1.

✓ You need to show your ability to find **explicit** (obvious) information in a text.

How long should I spend?

Spend about **5 minutes** on Question 1. Try not to spend longer as the later questions need more time.

For an explanation of what 'explicit information' is, go to page 8.

Top tips for success

✓ Read this question before you read Text 1, so you can find the information quickly.

✓ Don't write too much for each answer. Answer each part of the question in one phrase or sentence. Write each answer on the dotted line given for it.

✓ For this question, you can use short quotations or you can paraphrase (put the information in your own words).

Make sure that the answer you give connects to what the question is asking for. Read your answers carefully after you have written them.

Answering Question 1

Question 1 asks for obvious information and so it is a good chance to gain some straightforward marks at the beginning of the paper. Stay focused on the question and don't write more than you need to.

Steps to success

Read the question carefully. Make sure you understand what information the question is asking you to find.

1 Identify **four** <u>items that were on display</u> at the exhibition in the Crystal Palace.

(4 marks)

Make sure that each of your answers gives **different** information.

This is the information you need to find for this question.

2 Re-read the text to find four pieces of information that answer the question. For Question 1, you can look for the answers in the whole of Text 1.

As you read the text, you might find it useful to underline information that answers the question.

3 Check that all four of your answers directly respond to the question.

A quick check that you've actually answered the question will ensure that you don't lose valuable marks.

- -

Getting it right

1 'Splendid carriages of all kinds'.
2 'Railway engines'.
3 'Caskets full of real diamonds and pearls'.
4 'Mill machinery'.

In your answer book there will be a space specially for each answer.

You can put very short quotations for Question 1.

For Question 1, you don't need to write in full sentences. It's important that you simply write information that answers the question.

Understanding Question 2

Question 2 asks you to focus on specific lines of the source text, to make an evaluation, and to support your opinion with three reasons and examples.

How does Question 2 work?

Question 2 will tell you which lines in the text to focus on.

This is the **main focus** of this question. As you read the question, underline the main focus so you know what to look for.

Each of your three reasons should be supported by examples from the text.

> 2   In lines <u>1–8</u> the writer tries to help the reader <u>clearly imagine the Great Exhibition</u>.
>
> Evaluate how successfully this is achieved.
>
> Give **three** reasons for your opinion and use <u>examples</u> from lines 1–8.
>
> **(6 marks)**

You won't receive marks for examples taken from a different part of the text.

This question is worth 6 marks. Always check this so that you know how much you need to write.

An example can be a quotation, or you can paraphrase the text (put it in your own words). These examples should support the reasons you give in your answer.

What does Question 2 assess?

- ✓ Question 2 tests Assessment Objective 4.
- ✓ You need to show your ability to **evaluate** how successfully the writer has achieved the **main focus** of the question.
- ✓ You should offer your **own opinion** on the text.

Main focus – this will be the aspect of the text that the question asks about.

How much time should I spend?

You should spend between 10 and 12 minutes on Question 2.

Evaluate (verb)

To judge or calculate the importance, quantity or value of something.

E.g. At the end of the football season, the team evaluated their performance.

Synonyms: assess, appraise, judge, rate, weigh

What does 'evaluate' mean?

A useful way to think about evaluation is to look at **how well** something is achieved, rather than simply **how** it is achieved. For example, in the sample question, how well has the writer helped the reader to clearly imagine the Great Exhibition? You should discuss **how well** the writer has achieved this **overall**.

TOP TIP

Remember: In Question 2, you need to give three reasons, and each one must be supported with an example from the text.

Giving your own opinion

For evaluative questions, the examiners want to see you offer your **own opinion**. You can argue that the text is not successful, is partially successful, or is fully successful, as long as you **support your views** with **examples from the text**.

In 'evaluate' questions, you don't need to focus on the effects of the writer's techniques. For example, you could write 'the descriptions of the gold and silver add more detail to the text', and then you could explain why this helps the reader to imagine the Great Exhibition more clearly. You don't need to mention a writer's technique like a simile, hyperbole or personification.

Understanding Question 2

Read this page carefully to understand how to approach writing an answer to an **evaluative** question.

Extract taken from Charlotte Brontë's text describing the Great Exhibition. Find the full text on page 169.

Whatever human industry has created, you find there, from the great compartments filled with railway engines and boilers, with mill machinery in full work, with splendid carriages of all kinds, with harness of every description – to the glass-covered and velvet-spread stands loaded with the most gorgeous work of the goldsmith and silversmith, and the carefully guarded caskets full of real diamonds and pearls worth hundreds of thousands of pounds.

This list of different items helps the reader imagine the wide range of exhibits they could see.

The phrase 'splendid carriages of all kinds' conveys to the reader that there are lots of different items on display.

The words 'glass' and 'velvet' help the reader imagine textures and what the stands would feel like.

This phrase helps the reader to imagine something very beautiful.

Organising your answer

To keep your answer clear and focused on the question, you could use these useful phrases:

In my opinion, the text successfully / unsuccessfully / partially successfully … because …

First of all, … / Secondly, … / Thirdly, …

For example, the text states that …

This persuades the reader that … / The overall impression is that …

Begin your answer with an evaluative statement that makes clear your opinion of the text.

Introduce the reasons for your opinion.

Add an example from the text to support your reasons.

Offer a clear overall judgement of the text.

How is Question 2 marked?

Strong answers to Question 2:

- ✓ offer a critical evaluation – how well has the focus of the question been achieved?
- ✓ offer a convincing personal opinion – how successful did you think the text was?
- ✓ develop the evaluation by explaining why these examples show that the text is successful, or unsuccessful.
- ✓ remain focused on the question throughout.

TOP TIP

Top tips for success

- ✓ Make sure you understand the main focus of the question.
- ✓ Decide whether you find the text successful, unsuccessful or partially successful, and state this clearly.
- ✓ If you find the text unsuccessful or partially successful, make sure you clearly explain why.
- ✓ Give three reasons for your answer.
- ✓ Support each reason with an example from the text – either a quotation or a paraphrase.
- ✓ Explain clearly why your examples from the text support your evaluation.

Answering Question 2

You need to understand how you can write a successful answer to Question 2.

Reading the question

In lines 1–8 the writer tries to help the reader clearly imagine the Great Exhibition.

Evaluate how successfully this is achieved.

Give **three** reasons for your opinion and use examples <u>from lines 1–8</u>.

Always read the question carefully, so that you know what the topic of the question is. This will help you to remain focused on that as you write your answer.

Read this part of the question carefully. Don't use examples from anywhere else in the text.

Preparing to write your answer

✓ Re-read the section of the text that the question focuses on and underline key quotations you could use in your answer.

✓ Pick out three reasons why you think the text is successful, partially successful or unsuccessful.

✓ Make an overall judgement – how successfully has the focus been achieved?

Writing your answer

1 State your opinion on how successful the text is, and give your first reason, supported by an example from the text.

In my opinion, the writer successfully helps the reader to imagine the Great Exhibition, first by describing several of the exhibits on display.

Clearly state your opinion that you will support with reasons and examples in your answer.

2 Add an example from the text that supports your first reason.

For example, we learn about the 'railway engines and boilers', 'mill machinery in full work', and 'splendid carriages'.

Use quotation marks when you quote directly from the text.

3 Explain how this example supports your evaluation – how it demonstrates that the text is successful, or otherwise.

The detailed list of items on display helps the reader to visualise the exhibition and paints a clearer picture of what can be found there. The reader could almost imagine themselves walking between the different stands, taking in the 'mill machinery' and 'splendid carriages of all kinds'.

Show how the example you chose supports your opinion.

By adding further explanation, you can develop your answer and make it more convincing.

Answering Question 2

Getting it right

In my opinion, the text successfully helps the reader to imagine the exhibition. First of all, the writer tells us that 'whatever human industry has created, you find there'. This makes the exhibition seem like an interesting place to visit.

✓ The first sentence clearly expresses a personal opinion.

✗ The example of evidence doesn't fully support the point being made.

✗ This explanation doesn't respond to the main focus of the question.

I would argue that the text partially helps the reader to imagine the exhibition, because the writer does not describe all of the items on display. Firstly, the writer lists many of the items at the exhibition, such as the railway engines and boilers, and the 'work of the goldsmith and silversmith'. This helps the reader to appreciate the range of items that were on display. However, the writer does not describe in detail all of the items found in the exhibition: she doesn't tell us anything about what the 'mill machinery' or 'carriages' look like. This makes it harder for the reader to clearly imagine some parts of the exhibition at the Crystal Palace.

✓ The opening sentence offers a critical evaluation.

✓ This answer clearly explains why the text is successful.

✗ This answer could be improved by adding another point arguing why the text is successful.

✗ This point needs to be developed, to explain why it suggests that the text is not successful.

In my opinion, the writer successfully helps the reader to imagine the Great Exhibition. First of all, the writer lists many of the items on display, including machinery and precious stones, to give the reader a sense of the range of items they could see. She also tells us that the carriages were 'splendid' and the work of the goldsmiths was 'gorgeous' to convey to the reader how precious and attractive the exhibits were. The overall impression is to make the exhibition seem interesting and diverse, filled with many beautiful things to look at.

On the other hand, the writer tells us that the exhibition is 'impossible to describe', and she doesn't give much information about the Crystal Palace itself, or how the exhibition is organised. In my opinion, the writer gives the reader an impression of her experience, but doesn't help them to clearly imagine what it feels like to be in the halls of the Great Exhibition.

✓ This answer adds an additional point, to make a more persuasive argument.

✓ This clear evaluative sentence summarises the evaluation made in the paragraph.

✓ This answer provides a more critical evaluation, suggesting reasons why the text is not successful.

✓ This is an original and compelling evaluative point about the text.

Understanding Question 3

Question 3 will focus on the **language** that the writer uses and how it **interests** and **informs** the reader. You will have to use subject-specific terminology in your answer.

How does Question 3 work?

This is the focus of the question. As you read the text, think about how the writer uses language to keep the reader interested and informed.

As you read the text, think about how the writer uses language to make the reader think and feel something.

How does the writer use language to interest and inform the reader?

You should include:

- the writer's use of language
- the effect on the reader.

Use examples from the whole text and relevant subject terminology.

(8 marks)

For Question 3, you don't have to look at just one extract. You should include examples from the whole text in your answer.

Question 3 is worth more marks than Question 2. You should write more for this answer.

This includes word classes (noun, adjective, verb and adverb), and writer's techniques, such as similes, metaphors and personification.

What does Question 3 assess?

 Question 3 tests Assessment Objective 2.

 You need to show your ability to write about **how the writer uses language to interest and inform** the reader.

To 'inform' means to give information about a subject. As you read the text, pay attention to how the writer tries to **interest** the reader in the subject of the text, and how they try to keep the reader **informed**.

How much time should I spend?

Spend about 15 minutes on Question 3. Re-read the text carefully to find quotations and language features that you can discuss using subject terminology in your answer.

Using language to interest and inform the reader

... the glass-covered and velvet-spread stands loaded with the most gorgeous work of the goldsmith and silversmith

The writer informs the reader about the items on display by emphasising their beauty and value.

... none but supernatural hands could have arranged it thus, with such a blaze and contrast of colours ...

The writer attracts the reader's interest by creating a sense of awe – only a supernatural being could have organised the exhibition.

The writer interests the reader by making the exhibition seem striking and vivid.

The multitude filling the great aisles seems ruled and subdued by some invisible influence.

The writer informs the reader by giving the impression that the visitors were overcome with wonder.

Understanding Question 3

As well as writing about how the text interests and informs the reader, you need to use **relevant subject terminology** in your answer.

Using relevant subject terminology

Each of these quotations from Text 1 contains a language device that can be written about using subject terminology:

> <u>wonderful</u> place – vast, <u>strange</u>, <u>new</u> …

These adjectives interest the reader, emphasising that the exhibition will be unlike anything they have seen before.

> Amongst the thirty thousand souls that peopled it the day I was there, <u>not one loud noise was to be heard, not one irregular movement seen</u> …

The hyperbole informs the reader by suggesting that the crowd at the exhibition experienced wonder and awe.

> such a <u>blaze</u> and contrast of colours …

The noun 'blaze' has connotations of light and energy.

> the <u>living tide rolls on quietly</u>, with a deep hum like the sea heard from the distance.

This metaphor shows how the visitors were affected by visiting the exhibition. It gives the impression that they became unified by the experience of their visit.

To learn more about different language devices, turn to pages 14–19.

TOP TIP

Don't spend your time looking for a specific language device in the text, like a simile for example. There might not be one, and you'll waste valuable time. Instead, read the text to see which language devices the writer **has** used, and think about how these interest and inform the reader.

Writing about tone

As well as writing about language, you can also write about **tone**.

'Tone' means how the text sounds – this could be humorous, serious, factual or sarcastic. In this text, lines 11–15 are a good place to start when considering the tone of the text.

Charlotte Brontë writes that 'amongst the thirty thousand souls' that visited the exhibition there was 'not one loud noise … to be heard, not one irregular movement seen'. In these lines, the tone is hushed, awed and reverential. This informs the reader about the beauty and majesty of the exhibition.

To find out more about tone, look at page 19.

Using Point – Evidence – Explain

P–E–E is a useful technique for questions like Question 3 that ask you to write about the effect of the writer's language. You should use a range of phrases to link your point, evidence and explanation.

For more information on using P–E–E, go to page 48.

Answering Question 3

You need to understand how to write a good answer to Question 3.

Reading the question

3   How does the writer use language to interest and inform the reader?

You should include:

- the writer's use of language
- the effect on the reader.

Use examples from the whole text, and use relevant subject terminology.

(8 marks)

Question 3 will always ask you about how the writer uses language to interest and inform the reader.

You need to refer to the **whole** of Text 1 when you answer this question.

Preparing to write your answer

1 Read the text a second time and highlight or underline short quotations that you could use in your answer.

2 Choose which quotations you will use in your answer. Briefly annotate them, noting the language feature with relevant subject terminology, and the effect on the reader.

'a wonderful place – vast, strange, new ...'
- List of adjectives, interests the reader by making the exhibition seem unfamiliar.

Writing your answer

1

Make a **point** about the text.

First of all, the writer interests and informs the reader by describing the range of items on display in the exhibition.

2

Support the point with **evidence**.

For example, the writer lists the 'mill machinery', 'splendid carriages' and 'diamonds and pearls worth hundreds of thousands of pounds'.

This answer uses several short quotations to support the point.

3

Explain what this quotation makes the reader think and feel.

This list informs the reader about the sheer variety of different exhibits on display, giving the impression that the exhibition is full of fascinating sights. This helps to capture the reader's interest.

The student has identified 'list' as an example of subject terminology.

Here, they explain how the text would make the reader think and feel.

Answering Question 3

Getting it right

There are a number of ways that you can improve the quality of your response for Question 3.

The writer informs and interests the reader by making the Great Exhibition seem impressive and unusual. 'It is a wonderful place – vast, strange, new.' This emphasises that the Great Exhibition is impossible to describe.

✗ This quotation needs to be embedded into a sentence.

✗ Here, the student could explain in more detail how this quotation would affect the reader.

The writer gets the reader interested in the exhibition by making it seem highly impressive, and almost magical. The references to 'magic' and 'supernatural hands' suggests to the reader that this is an awe-inspiring place. In addition, the description of the 'blaze and contrast of colours' further grabs the reader's attention, allowing them to vividly imagine the scene being described.

✓ The opening sentence clearly explains the effect the writer has created.

✗ This answer needs to refer to relevant subject terminology.

✗ The answer could be improved by adding another point, with phrases like 'in addition' and 'furthermore'.

In this extract, the writer informs and interests the reader by expressing the wonder she experienced whilst visiting the Great Exhibition. She writes that it was as if only 'supernatural hands' could have arranged the exhibition, and this interests the reader by emphasising how different the exhibition was from the outside world. The writer also notes that the visitors to the exhibition seemed 'ruled and subdued by some invisible influence'. The verbs 'ruled' and 'subdued' tell the reader about the impact that the exhibition had on the visitors, and give the impression that the visitors were overcome with wonder. In addition, the noun phrase 'some invisible influence' makes the reader imagine a supernatural power. This would make the reader even more interested in the exhibition as this gives the impression that the Great Exhibition is completely different from the ordinary world.

✓ The first sentence explains the effect the writer is trying to create.

✓ The student uses short, relevant quotations, and explains their effect.

✓ The student supports their points with relevant subject terminology.

✓ Further explanation is added with the phrase 'in addition'.

Understanding Question 4a

Question 4 will focus on the second exam text, Text 2. Make sure you understand how this question works and what it is asking you to do.

How does Question 4 work?

Question 4 will be divided into part a and part b.

Read the question carefully. Make sure you understand what information you need to look for.

For information on Question 4b, turn to page 75.

This question asks you to look for information in specific lines. You should look for the answers only in this part of the text.

4a From lines 10–19, identify **two** things that spectators in the crowd did.

(2 marks)

Question 4a will always ask you to find two different pieces of explicit information. 'Explicit information' is directly stated in the text.

For Question 4, 2 marks are awarded for part a, and 2 marks for part b.

What does Question 4a assess?

☑ Question 4a tests Assessment Objective 1.

☑ You need to show your ability to find explicit information and ideas.

How is Question 4a marked?

☑ For part a, **one mark** is available for **each** answer.

How long should I spend?

You should spend about 5–8 minutes in total on Questions 4a and 4b. Leave yourself time for the next questions, which will take longer.

Explicit information

Like Question 1, Question 4a **asks you only to look for explicit information and ideas.** You don't need to look for hidden meanings. You don't need to explain what you find. You just need to find short quotations or paraphrase (put into your own words) what is clearly there.

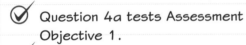

TOP TIP

Use short quotations that contain the information you need for the answer. Don't spend too much time writing down long quotations.

Paper 1: linked theme

Text 1 and Text 2 in these Paper 1 exam skills pages are each about a different spectacle in 19th-century London. In your Paper 1 exam, you will have two texts on a linked theme. Your writing question (see page 85) will also link to this theme.

See page 9 for more detail on explicit information.

Answering Question 4a

Like Question 1, Question 4a only asks you to look for explicit information. This gives you the chance to gain some straightforward marks before moving on to the next questions.

Steps to success

1

Read the question carefully. Make sure you understand what information the question is asking you to find.

4a From lines 10–19, identify **two** things that spectators in the crowd did.

Make sure that your answers come only from the lines specified in the question.

2

Re-read the text to find two pieces of information to quote or put into your own words.

Write each answer on the line given for it.

1 Some people fainted.
2 They 'flocked on to the ground'.

The text says that some women were 'swooning': here the student has paraphrased the text (put it into their own words).

3

Check that both of your answers directly respond to the question.

1 There were fights between members of the crowd.
2 Some women were 'swooning'.

As with Question 1, you don't need to answer in a full sentence for Question 4a. It's important that you give information that answers the question, such as the examples given here.

You can quote from the text or paraphrase the ideas. If you paraphrase the text, you need to do it accurately, and respond directly to the question.

Keep your answers short and relevant.

Getting it right

1 The spectators used bad language.
2 Their 'cries and howls' were shrill.

✗ This information is in line 8 whereas the question relates to text in lines 10–19.

✗ The text does say this but the answer doesn't directly address the question of what the spectators did.

1 The spectators let out shrill 'cries and howls'.
2 They made unkind jokes.

✓ This answer directly addresses the question.

✓ This answers the question by paraphrasing the text.

Understanding Question 4b

Question 4b gives you an extract from the text and asks you to identify information in it.

How does Question 4b work?

b   Read this extract.

> When the sun rose brightly it [shone upon] thousands upon thousands of upturned faces, so inexpressibly odious in their brutal mirth or callousness, that a man had cause to feel ashamed of the shape he wore, and to shrink from himself, as fashioned in the image of the Devil.
>
> When the two miserable [criminals] who attracted all this ghastly sight about them were turned into the air, there was no more emotion, no more restraint in any of the previous obscenities, than if the name of Christ had never been heard in this world, and there were no belief among men but that they perished like the beasts.

From the extract, identify **two** things that tell us that the spectators did not feel pity towards the criminals who were executed.

(2 marks).

Question 4b will ask you to read a short section of the text. This will be printed on the same page as the question.

Question 4b will always ask you to find two different pieces of information.

This is the topic of the question. Read it carefully so you understand what information to look for.

There are 2 marks available for Question 4a, and 2 for Question 4b.

What does Question 4b assess?

✓ Question 4b tests Assessment Objective 1.
✓ You need to show your ability to interpret implicit information and ideas.

How much time should I spend?

Remember that you should spend around 5–8 minutes in total on Questions 4a and 4b. Don't spend too long, as the later questions will need more time.

What are 'implicit information and ideas'?

Implicit information is not directly stated in the text. You will have to work out what the writer is suggesting or implying. This is also called **making an inference** or **reading between the lines**.

See page 10 for more detail on implicit information and ideas.

How is Question 4b marked?

 For part b, **one mark** is available for **each** answer you give.
 You will gain a mark for a reasonable answer – an example of implicit information that makes sense.

Top tips for success

TOP TIP

✓ Read Question 4b carefully so you know what information to look for.
✓ Read the extract carefully, to identify the implicit information and ideas.
✓ Only give 2 answers. You won't improve the quality of your response by including more.
✓ Keep your answers concise – don't write more than you need to and put each answer on the numbered lines in the paper.

Answering Question 4b

You need to understand how you can write a good answer to Question 4b.

Reading the text extract

Look in the extract for words and phrases that **imply** or **suggest** something.

When the sun rose brightly it [shone upon] thousands upon thousands of upturned faces, so inexpressibly odious in their <u>brutal mirth</u> or callousness, that a man had cause to feel ashamed of the shape he wore, and to shrink from himself, as fashioned in the image of the Devil.

When the two miserable [criminals] who attracted all this ghastly sight about them were turned into the air, there was no more emotion, <u>no more restraint in any of the previous obscenities</u>, than if the name of Christ had never been heard in this world, and there were no belief among men but that <u>they perished like the beasts</u>.

The phrase 'brutal mirth' implies humour.

This implies that the crowd did not improve their behaviour.

This suggests that the criminals were seen only as animals, not human beings.

Getting it right

1 The phrase 'brutal mirth' suggests that the crowd found the execution funny.

2 After the execution, there was 'no more restraint in any of the previous obscenities'.

✓ Your inferences should be reasonable and convincing.

✓ Show that you understand what is implied by the evidence you choose.

✓ You can paraphrase the text, or use a quotation.

1 The crowd did not change their behaviour once the two criminals had been executed.

2 The crowd believed that the criminals 'perished like the beasts'.

Try to use correct spelling and punctuation in your answer.

Understanding Question 5

Question 5 will always be structured in the same way. Make sure you understand how this question works and what it is asking you to do.

How does Question 5 work?

5   Read this extract.

> I am solemnly convinced that nothing that ingenuity could devise to be done in this city could work such ruin as one public execution, and I stand astounded and appalled by the wickedness it exhibits. I do not believe that any community can prosper where such a scene of horror and demoralization as was enacted outside Horsemonger-lane Jail is presented at the very doors of good citizens, and is passed by, unknown or forgotten. And when, in our prayers and thanksgivings for the season, we are humbly expressing before God our desire to remove the moral evils of the land, I would ask your readers to consider whether it is not a time to think of this one, and to root it out.

In the extract the writer tries to persuade the reader that executions should not be held in public.

Evaluate how successfully this is achieved.

Give **three** reasons for your opinion and use examples from the extract.

(6 marks)

Question 5 will ask you to read a section (an extract) of Text 2. This will be printed on the same page as the question.

The word 'persuade' lets you know the writer's purpose in this text. Some other words that show a writer's purpose might include 'argue', 'show', 'demonstrate', 'convince' or 'advise'.

This is the main focus of the question. You need to decide how successfully the writer has persuaded the reader of this.

Check how many marks the question is worth. This will help you to manage your time.

What does Question 5 assess?

✓ Question 5 tests Assessment Objective 4.

✓ You need to be able to evaluate how successful the writer is in achieving the aim of their writing.

✓ You should develop your own informed opinion about how well the writer has achieved their purpose in the extract.

How much time should I spend? ⏱

Spend about 10–12 minutes on Question 5. Make sure you leave enough time for Question 6, which will take longer.

In this question you should consider how effectively the writer manages to persuade his readers. You might decide that the writer is successful, unsuccessful or partially successful, and you must always support your opinions with evidence.

Writing to persuade, show or argue

In many texts, writers will try to show you that their viewpoint is correct. This is sometimes called writing to persuade, show or argue. As you read the extract for Question 5, you should consider how successfully the writer 'shows' or 'persuades' you that their beliefs are true.

Understanding Question 5

Writers often use a range of techniques when trying to convince their readers of something. Learn to recognise these techniques and discuss their impact in your answer.

The purpose of the text

Here are some extracts from the text about the execution, in which the writer is trying to persuade readers.

> I am solemnly convinced that <u>nothing that ingenuity could devise</u> to be done in this city could work such ruin as one public execution, and I stand astounded and appalled by the wickedness it exhibits.

The writer makes a clear, unambiguous statement to show his readers how strongly he feels.

The exaggerated statement emphasises the seriousness of this issue.

> I do not believe that any community can prosper where such <u>a scene of horror and demoralization</u> as was enacted outside Horsemonger-lane Jail …

The emotive language creates a strong emotional response in the reader, helping to convince them that public executions are wrong.

> And when, in <u>our</u> prayers and thanksgivings for the season, <u>we</u> are humbly expressing before God our desire to remove the moral evils of the land …

The words 'we' and 'our' create a sense that the writer and the readers are united and share common goals.

How is Question 5 marked?

Strong answers to Question 5:

✓ evaluate how successfully the writer has achieved their aims

✓ give convincing personal opinions on how well the focus of the question has been achieved

✓ use relevant examples from the text, including short quotations that fully support the evaluation being made.

Useful evaluative language

Make sure you are using evaluative language in your answer.

> Overall, the text successfully persuades the reader that …
>
> The text consistently …
>
> In general, the text …
>
> In my opinion, the text succeeds in …

TOP TIP

Top tips for success

✓ Make a judgement, and clearly state how well you feel the focus of the question has been achieved.

✓ Use language for giving opinions, such as 'I think …', 'I feel …' and 'I would argue that … because …'.

✓ Give **three** reasons for your opinion.

✓ Support each reason with an example, either by paraphrasing the text or by giving a quotation.

✓ Explain clearly how your examples from the text support your opinion.

Answering Question 5

You need to understand how to write a successful answer to Question 5.

Reading the question

In the exam, the whole extract will be printed on the same page as the question.

5   Read this extract.

> I am solemnly convinced that … and to root it out.

In this extract, the writer tries to persuade the reader that executions should not be held in public.

Evaluate how successfully this is achieved.

Give **three** reasons for your opinion and use examples from the extract.

(6 marks)

Read the extract carefully. Make sure you understand the writer's ideas and viewpoint.

Check what the question is asking. Look for key words such as 'persuade'.

You need to give three reasons for your opinion about the success of the writing.

Question 5 will always be very similar to Question 2 (see pages 65–68). The questions will focus on different texts, but both will ask you to 'evaluate' an extract, and support your opinion with three examples from the text.

Preparing to write your answer

- Re-read the section of the text that the question focuses on and underline three key quotations you could use in your answer.

- Make a judgement – how well has the focus of the question been achieved?

Writing your answer

1

State your opinion on how successful the text is, and give your first reason, supported by an example from the text.

I believe that the writer successfully persuades the reader that public executions should be banned. First of all, the writer tells the reader that he is 'astounded and appalled by the wickedness' that public executions produce in the onlooking crowd.

Use signposts like 'first of all' and 'secondly' to introduce your three points.

Give your example using quotations or paraphrasing.

2

Explain how this example supports your evaluation – how it demonstrates that the text is successful, or otherwise.

The words 'astounded' and 'appalled' demonstrate the strength of the writer's feelings, and help to persuade the reader that public executions clearly have a negative impact on those watching.

Keep your answer focused on the question by explaining how the quotation links to the focus of the question. You may also find it useful to repeat key words from the question, such as 'persuade', in your answer.

Answering Question 5

Read the answers on this page to understand how to improve the quality of your response for Question 5.

Getting it right

In this extract, the writer uses several emotive words like 'appalled' and 'horror'. He also writes that 'nothing that ingenuity could devise to be done in this city could work such ruin as one public execution'. This emphasises to the reader how destructive public executions can be.

✗ You won't receive marks for comments about subject terminology without also evaluating its impact.

✗ You need to give three reasons for your opinion.

In this extract, the writer successfully persuades his readers that public executions should be forbidden. First of all, he uses emotive words such as 'wickedness' and 'horror' to describe the effect of public executions and show the reader how strongly he feels. Secondly, he writes that 'nothing … could work such ruin as one public execution', demonstrating the clearly negative effect that public executions have. Finally, he discusses himself and his readers as one group, using language such as 'we' and 'our'. This helps to persuade the readers that they are all one group, with the same objective: in this case, abolishing public executions.

✓ This answer opens with a clear evaluative statement.

✗ This comment does not explain how the use of emotive language persuades the reader. The student could continue with 'the readers will find themselves influenced by his use of emotive language'.

In my opinion, the writer persuasively argues that executions should not be held in public. He opens the text with a clear, emphatic statement of his views: he is 'solemnly convinced' of the evil of public execution. His certainty helps to reassure the reader that his opinion on public punishments is correct. Secondly, he writes about himself and his readers as one group, who 'in our prayers and thanksgivings' are 'humbly expressing … our desire to remove the moral evils of the land'. The use of the words 'we' and 'our' makes the readers feel united, and that they have a shared goal – removing the evil of public execution. Finally, the writer appeals to his readers' desire for a better world by stating that he doesn't believe that 'any community can prosper' whilst public executions take place, and that events like this work 'ruin'. The overall impact, created through a range of persuasive devices, is to inspire the readers that London would be a better city if public executions were outlawed.

✓ This answer makes an effective point about the structure of the paragraph and its impact.

✓ Here the student makes an insightful and original point.

✓ The concluding evaluative point summarises the arguments made in the answer.

74

Understanding Question 6

Question 6 asks you to refer to the whole of Text 2. You need to evaluate the text in light of an opinion given in the question.

How does Question 6 work?

Question 6 will always ask you to consider the whole of Text 2 in your answer.

Make sure you use examples from the whole text.

> 6   For this question refer to the whole of Text 2.
>
> 'In my view, this text shows how violent spectacles can bring out the worst in people.'
>
> Based on your evaluation of the text, how far do you agree with this opinion?
>
> Use examples from the text to support your evaluation.
>
> (12 marks)

This exam question will include an interpretation of Text 2. This interpretation will always be given in quotation marks.

This is the main focus of the question. Read this carefully so you know what to write about in your answer.

Question 6 carries the most marks for Section A. You will need to write more for this answer, and allow yourself enough time.

What does Question 6 assess?

- ✓ Question 6 tests Assessment Objective 4.
- ✓ You need to show you can respond to another opinion on the text, and decide how far you agree.
- ✓ You should explain how far you agree with the opinion, and support your point of view with examples from the text.
- ✓ You will have to base your response to the opinion in the question on your own evaluation of the text.

How much time should I spend?

Spend about 18 minutes on Question 6.

This question is worth 12 marks so leave yourself enough time to answer it well. However, don't spend too much time on it – you'll need enough time to complete the writing task in Section B.

Responding to an interpretation

Question 6 will always include an interpretation (someone else's opinion of the text). Based on your evaluation of the text, you will have to explain how far you agree with the interpretation given in the question.

Remember, to **evaluate** something means to give an **overall judgement**, or determine **how successfully something has been achieved**.

For the question on this page, you have to evaluate how well you think the text demonstrates that violent spectacles can bring out the worst in people.

Useful language

You could use any of the following phrases when responding to an interpretation.

> On the whole, I agree with this interpretation because ...
>
> I wholeheartedly agree with this point of view ...
>
> I partly agree with this opinion ...
>
> In my opinion, this statement accurately summarises the text ...

Understanding Question 6

Stepping back – looking at the text as a whole

Question 6 will ask you to evaluate Text 2 as a whole. This means you will have an opportunity both to focus on the general themes and ideas in the text, and to look at individual quotations and short sections.

You should use a mixture of quotations and paraphrasing (putting the text in your own words) as evidence to support your answer.

You don't need to use specialist subject terminology in your answer to Question 6. You do not need to write about the writer's techniques (such as similes and metaphors) or word classes (such as adjectives, nouns and verbs). If you do mention writing techniques, you need to discuss how well they contribute to the overall impact of the text.

General themes and ideas are the big, overarching ideas that the writer explores in the text. In Text 2, a general theme is the bad behaviour that is sparked by public executions.

How is Question 6 marked?

Strong answers to Question 6:

✓ offer a convincing personal judgement on the text

✓ offer a well developed critical evaluation of the text

✓ use appropriate and relevant examples from the text that fully support the points being made

✓ remain focused on the question throughout.

See page 12 for more on tone and structure.

Structure and tone

As you have to discuss the whole of Text 2, Question 6 could be a good opportunity to discuss the impact of **structure** and **tone**. 'Structure' means how the text is organised, and which information is given at which point. '**Tone**' refers to how the text sounds – **shocked, sarcastic, dispassionate** or **humorous**, for example.

Consider the tone and structure of Text 2, and decide how effective they make the text at achieving its objectives.

TOP TIP

Top tips for success

✓ Plan your answer to help you stay focused on the question.

✓ Start by stating clearly how far you agree with the interpretation.

✓ Use clear and relevant examples to support your opinion.

✓ Give your answer a clear and logical structure – use P–E–E paragraphs, for example.

✓ You do not need to refer to the writer's techniques. If you do, make sure you say how they affect the overall impact of the text.

Answering Question 6

You need to understand how you can write a successful answer to Question 6.

Reading the question

6   For this question refer to the whole of Text 2.

'In my view, this text shows how violent spectacles can bring out the worst in people.'

Based on your evaluation of the text, how far do you agree with this opinion?

Use examples from the text to support your evaluation.

(12 marks)

Remember to consider the whole of Text 2, not just one extract, for Question 6.

Read the interpretation carefully. Check you understand it before reading the text and deciding how far you agree.

Question 6 carries the most marks in Section A. Make sure you give yourself enough time to answer it properly.

Steps to success

1   Re-read and annotate the text, looking for ideas and quotations you could use in your evaluation.

Remember that for evaluative questions it can be useful to paraphrase the text or focus on the general ideas.

2   Make a judgement – how persuasive do you find the text?

How successfully does the text show that violent spectacles bring out the worst in people?

Don't be afraid to disagree with the interpretation in the question if you feel you can persuasively support your opinion.

3   Plan your answer before writing.

Paragraph 1
Opening sentence – strongly agree with interpretation.
General tone – shocked, even horrified.
Strong language – 'awful', 'wickedness', 'horror'.
Intended to show how awful the behaviour was that the writer saw.

Paragraph 2
Indifference towards suffering.
'they perished like the beasts'.
The violent spectacle bringing out unhealthy emotions, not positive ones.

Paragraph 3
Effects of violent spectacles on a city or community.
Public executions work 'such ruin' – suggests destruction.
Communities can't 'prosper'.
Violent spectacles bring out the worst in cities, not just crowds.

The plan for each paragraph should show how the answer will continuously focus on the question.

Your plan should help you clearly state your evaluation – how successfully you think the text persuades you.

Answering Question 6

Getting it right

I strongly agree that this text shows how violent spectacles bring out the worst in people. First of all, the writer uses a shocked, horrified tone throughout the text, using words such as 'wickedness', 'horror' and 'demoralization'. Then, we learn that the crowd carried on with their bad behaviour even when the people were hanged. This shows that violent spectacles bring out the worst in people. Finally, the writer tells us that public executions have a negative impact on a whole city, further showing how violent spectacles bring out the worst in people.

✓ The student is using examples from the whole text.

✗ This point would be stronger with further explanation: how does the horrified tone help to show the reader that violent spectacles bring out the worst in people?

✗ This sentence doesn't add any new information or explanation.

✗ This point needs evidence from the text.

I strongly agree that this text shows how violent spectacles bring out the worst in people. First of all, the tone of the text is shocked, even horrified, as the writer describes the behaviour he witnessed in the crowd. The writer uses very strong words – he describes the 'wickedness' of the crowd as 'inconceivably awful', and later describes the scene as one of 'horror and demoralization'. Through this horrified tone, the writer conveys to the reader just how awful the behaviour was that he witnessed that night, and demonstrates that violent spectacles like public executions bring out the worst in people.

This text also shows how violent spectacles bring out a crowd's indifference towards suffering. After the two criminals had died, 'there was … no more restraint in any of the previous obscenities', and the crowd believed that the criminals 'perished like the beasts'. Rather than feeling sympathy towards the criminals, the crowd feel only indifferent and uncaring towards them. As these are clearly not healthy, positive emotions, it seems clear that a violent spectacle like an execution brings out the worst in people.

Finally, the writer discusses the wider impact on a city that the violent spectacle of a public execution has. He writes that nothing could be done in the city to work such 'ruin' as a public execution. The word 'ruin' suggests just how destructive these events are. Furthermore, he argues that no city can 'prosper' when violent spectacles are allowed to happen, implying that his city is not 'prospering'. Earlier in the text, the writer shows how the city is not 'prospering', by describing the shocking behaviour, like fighting and brutal jokes, that happens at a public execution. In my opinion, this shows how violent spectacles bring out the worst not just in crowds or individuals, but in communities and cities. For these reasons, I strongly agree with the interpretation in the question.

✓ This paragraph begins with a clear topic sentence.

✓ This answer makes an effective point about the writer's tone, and explains how it helps show the negative impact of violent spectacles.

✓ The student links their point back to the opinion in the question.

✓ This paragraph is also strengthened by giving more than one example from the text.

✓ The student makes an interesting and original point, still linked back to the question.

Understanding Section B

How does Section B work?

Section B will include Question 7 and Question 8. You have to **choose one** of these questions to answer.

This is the genre (type) of text you will write. Check this carefully so you know how to structure and organise the writing task.

This is the topic of the task. Read this carefully so that your answer responds to the task.

For Question 7 writing tasks, the opening sentences will be given to you. Use these as a starting point, and continue writing.

EITHER

*7 Write a speech for sixteen-year-olds with the title 'Why young people should visit museums, art galleries and exhibitions'.

A student has started a response to this task.

Nowadays, there is an enormous range of exhibitions and museums to choose from, including art galleries, history museums, and even exhibitions on food and fashion! But why should you spend your weekends checking out the local art gallery? In this speech, I'd like to tell you why.

Continue this speech using your own ideas (do not copy information from Texts 1 and 2).

You can use Texts 1 and 2 for ideas. But you must **not** copy from the texts directly.

OR

*8 Write a letter to the headteacher of your school with an idea for a school trip to a museum or exhibition you'd like to organise.

You should include:

- what museum you'd like to visit
- how the school trip will be a beneficial educational experience
- other ways that the school trip will benefit the students.

Your response will be marked for the accurate and appropriate use of vocabulary, spelling, punctuation and grammar.

(40 marks)

Question 8 will give you a list of points to include in your answer. You need to write about each point.

In Section B, you will be rewarded for using ambitious vocabulary and for varying your punctuation and sentence structure.

Section B is worth half of the marks for Paper 1. Make sure you leave yourself enough time to answer it.

What does Section B assess?

☑ Section B tests Assessment Objectives 5 and 6.

☑ AO5 tests your ability to communicate clearly and imaginatively, and to adapt your language, tone and content to suit the writing task and audience.

☑ AO6 tests your ability to use a range of vocabulary and sentence structures, and accurate spelling, punctuation and grammar.

How much time should I spend?

You should spend around 45 minutes on Section B. Spend 5–10 minutes planning, and 30–35 minutes writing. You should leave some time at the end to check your work.

Understanding Section B

Make sure you understand what your chosen question in Section B is asking you to do.

What will I have to write for Section B?

In Section B, you will be given a choice of two tasks from a range of possible genres (types of text). These include letters, articles, reports, speeches, reviews, formal emails or blogs.

Each writing task will require you to adapt your language, structure and tone to meet the requirements of each genre. For example, to write a letter you will have to open and close the letter correctly, and select a tone appropriate to the person you're writing to. To write a report you should write in a formal tone, and you could make use of statistics and facts. Make sure you are familiar with each of the possible genres, and the style and structure you should use for each one.

To learn more about different writing genres, see pages 30–32.

SPaG

You will be marked on the accuracy of your spelling, grammar and punctuation for Section B. You should read through your work to check it after you finish.

You will also be marked on how ambitious and varied your **vocabulary, punctuation** and **sentence structure** are.

Punctuation: Use colons, exclamation marks, semicolons and question marks.

Sentence structure: Use a range of long and short sentences, and sentences with subordinate clauses.

Vocabulary: Think of unusual and creative adjectives, adverbs and verbs that you can use in your answer.

Turn to pages 57–59 to find more on spelling. To learn more about different types of punctuation, see pages 53–61.

Who is my audience?

The writing task for Section B will tell you who the **audience** or **readers** of your text will be. For example, you could be asked to write an article for a teen magazine that suggests different ways to keep healthy. You should adapt the language and content of your text to suit your audience.

Each writing task will have a **purpose:** something you will have to achieve in the text. For example, it could be persuading young people to do more exercise, or providing a report on the sports facilities available in your town.

As you plan and write your response, make sure that you are achieving the purpose of the task.

How is Section B marked?

Strong answers to Section B:

- ☑ are well organised, with introductory and concluding paragraphs
- ☑ feature a range of ambitious vocabulary, varied punctuation and sentence structures
- ☑ fulfil the purpose of the task, and respond to the needs and interests of the readers or audience
- ☑ will be imaginative and interesting to read.

Top tips for success

TOP TIP

- ✓ Plan your answer before you start writing.
- ✓ Make sure that you fulfil the requirements of your chosen writing task. If you're writing a formal letter, use the appropriate tone. If you're writing a speech, address your audience directly.
- ✓ Write about three paragraphs, and an opening and concluding paragraph.
- ✓ Check that you're using a range of punctuation and sentence structures.

Answering Section B

You need to understand how you can write a successful answer for Section B.
This and the next page deal with answers for sample Question 7 only.

Reading the question

*7   Write a <u>speech for sixteen-year-olds</u> with the title
    '<u>Why young people should visit museums, art</u>
    <u>galleries and exhibitions</u>'.

    A student has started a response to this task.

    *Nowadays, there is an enormous range of exhibitions
    and museums to choose from, including art galleries,
    history museums, and even exhibitions on food and
    fashion! But why should you spend your weekends
    checking out the local art gallery? In this speech, I'd
    like to tell you why.*

    Continue this speech, using your own ideas (do not
    copy information from Texts 1 and 2).

    *Your response will be marked for the accurate and
    appropriate use of vocabulary, spelling, punctuation
    and grammar.*

                                                (40 marks)

Make sure you know the type of text, and who the audience will be.

Make sure you understand the purpose of the task. Your answer should be focused on this throughout.

You don't need to copy out the given introductory sentences. You can continue the task from where they end.

Section B is worth half of the marks for Paper 1. You should spend about 45 minutes on this section.

Planning your answer

You should use the space provided in the exam booklet to plan your answer.

Your plan should help you to structure your answer. You should note the general ideas that you will cover in each paragraph.

Purpose – persuade audience to visit exhibitions, galleries, museums
Audience – teenagers – informal tone, exclamation marks
Genre – speech – address audience directly, finish with call to action

Paragraph 1
• Visiting museums and exhibitions will enrich your life.
• Opportunity to learn something new; find a new hobby.
• This might give ideas for future job or studies.

Paragraph 2
• How do you begin choosing an exhibition to visit?
• Make a list of topics that already interest you or that you'd like to learn more about.
• Look at ads on social media, and posters in bus and train stations.
• Finally, don't be afraid to try something new!

Paragraph 3
• Personal anecdote about visiting exhibition.
• Finish speech with call to action – inspire students to go out and enrich their lives.

You might find it useful to note down the audience, purpose and genre, so that you consistently meet the requirements of the writing task.

This plan demonstrates how the student will organise each paragraph, developing their ideas and using persuasive devices such as rhetorical questions and a personal anecdote.

Answering Section B

Getting it right

There are a number of ways you can improve the quality of your response for Section B.

The first reason why you should visit museums, exhibitions and galleries is that they will enrich your life. Exhibitions and museums are a fantastic place to learn something new, about history, about science, about other cultures – even about new sports and hobbies! You might visit the Natural History Museum in London, and find yourself enthralled by prehistoric remains. Or perhaps an exhibition on Bollywood will give you a love of jazz and hip-hop dance. Expanding your horizons and learning about different aspects of culture will enrich your life for years to come. Who knows, perhaps you'll discover a subject you'd like to study at university, or even your future profession!

So, how do you go about choosing an exhibition to visit? First of all, make a list of topics and hobbies you find interesting. Perhaps you're into Indian cuisine, or Japanese anime, or maybe you'd like to learn more about what life was like during the Second World War. You could even write down topics you know nothing about, but would love to discover: how does the human eye work, for example? Or what was it like to be a child during the Victorian era? Making a list of possible topics will help you to narrow down your search, and find the exhibitions that will captivate you. (You may not want to waste your time at an exhibition on different types of plastic!) And of course if you're not sure that a museum is right for you, why not just give it a go? The worst that can happen is that you're yawning for half an hour, and then you go and buy an ice cream from the cafeteria!

Let me tell you about an exhibition that expanded my world. I once saw an advert on social media for an exhibition on sci-fi, fantasy, and horror films. My first thoughts were dragons, aliens, bad CGI – that's not really my thing. But I went along ... and I was entranced. I loved the pictures of the bizarre alien landscapes, the life-size cut-outs of grotesque and terrifying monsters, the fascinating range of props and costumes from hundreds of different films. I ended up staying there for over three hours! If I hadn't gone to the exhibition, I don't think I would have applied to study film at university, and wouldn't have discovered my dream – to design props for films. So, to conclude, I'd like to tell you: expand your horizons! Visit an exhibition! Try something new! You might learn about something that will alter the direction of your life.

Thanks for listening!

✓ The main body of the speech begins with a clear topic sentence.

✓ This speech features ambitious vocabulary like 'enthralled' and phrases like 'expanding your horizons'.

✓ The examples of different exhibitions add detail and make this speech more interesting.

✓ The content is consistently relevant for a teenage audience.

✓ Another topic sentence helps the audience to know what this next point is about.

✓ The informal tone is appropriate to the task and audience.

✓ The range of punctuation and varied sentence structure make this answer pleasant and engaging to listen to.

✓ The anecdote (short personal story) makes the speech more relatable, and helps the audience to connect with the speaker.

✓ The tone changes in this paragraph, becoming more serious to reflect the speaker's emotions as they visited the exhibition.

✓ The short, imperative (command) sentences are a direct and inspiring call to action.

✓ The speech concludes by tempting the audience to look forwards to what might happen if they take up the call to action.

 **Time**

Spend about **5 minutes** on Question 1.

Unlocking the question

You need to find four pieces of **explicit** information.

Watch out!

All of your answers need to be short and directly respond to the question.

Hint

You can use a short quotation or paraphrase the text.

Time

Spend about **10–12 minutes** on Question 2.

Unlocking the question

Check you understand the main focus of the question before you begin your answer.

Unlocking the question

Question 2 asks you to **evaluate**: you need to decide how successfully the writer has achieved their aims.

Hint

Choose your three reasons **before** you begin your answer.

English Language 2.0
Paper 1: Non-Fiction Texts

SECTION A

Reading

You should spend about 1 hour 10 minutes on this section.

Read Text 1 in the Source Booklet provided and answer Questions 1–3.

Write your answers in the spaces provided.

1   Identify **four** difficulties that children from the Ragged School face.

(4 marks)

1 ....

2 ....

3 ....

4 ....

2   In lines 1–12, the writer encourages the reader to feel sympathy for the ragged children.

Evaluate how successfully this is achieved.

Give **three** reasons for your opinion and use examples from lines 1–12.

(6 marks)

....

....

....

....

....

....

....

....

(blank lined answer space)

Watch out!

Write only about the lines specified in the question.

Unlocking the question

Read the extract and make a judgement on how successfully the writer has achieved their aims.

Hint

Start by clearly stating how successful you think the text is.

Hint

Use evaluative language, such as 'the text successfully persuades the reader that', and 'the text makes clear that'.

Hint

Use language that makes it clear that you are giving your own opinion, such as 'in my opinion', and 'I feel'.

LEARN IT!

Structure your answer clearly. Use a separate P–E–E (point, evidence, explanation) paragraph for each reason.

Watch out!

Make sure you explain why each example supports your opinion.

Hint

Paraphrasing the text can be very useful for evaluate questions.

Hint

Clearly signpost your reasons, using language such as 'first of all', 'secondly' and 'in addition'.

Time

Spend about **15 minutes** on Question 3.

Unlocking the question

For Question 3, you are being asked to look closely at the writer's use of language, including the writer's techniques, word classes and tone.

Hint

Before you answer, underline and annotate short quotations you could use in your answer.

Unlocking the question

You need to explain what the writer's language makes the reader **think** and **feel**.

Hint

Question 3 is an excellent opportunity to focus closely on short quotations and individual words.

Watch out!

You need to use subject terminology in your answer, such as for word classes (e.g. adjective, noun, verb) and writers' techniques (e.g. hyperbole, simile).

3 How does the writer use language to interest and inform the reader?

You should include:

- the writer's use of language
- the effect on the reader.

Use examples from the whole text and relevant subject terminology.

(8 marks)

....

....

....

....

....

....

....

....

....

....

....

....

....

....

....

....

....

....

....

....

....

....

....

....

....

....

....

....

....

....

....

....

....

....

....

....

....

....

....

....

....

....

....

....

....

....

....

If you need more space for your answers, continue writing on your own
separate pieces of paper.

LEARN IT!

Use P–E–E paragraphs
to structure your answer.
Quote and paraphrase
from the text, and clearly
explain how the language
impacts the reader.

Watch out!

Don't waste time copying
down long quotations
when a shorter quotation
would be more effective.

Hint

Use phrases for
discussing the impact of
language, such as 'this
gives the impression
that...', 'this implies...',
and 'the effect of
this is...'.

Hint

Pay attention to the
tone of the text and the
writer's language, and
how these affect what
the reader thinks
and feels.

Watch out!

Questions 4–6 are about
Text 2.

Time

Spend about **2–3
minutes** on Question 4a.

**Unlocking
the question**

Question 4a will always
ask you to look for
explicit (directly stated)
information.

**Unlocking
the question**

Check you understand
the main focus of
the question.

Hint

Use short quotations or
paraphrasing for
this question.

Time

Spend around **5 minutes**
on Question 4b.

**Unlocking
the question**

Question 4b will always
ask you to look for **implicit
information and ideas**.

**Unlocking
the question**

For Question 4b, you
need to show that you
understand the implicit
meaning of the quotations
you choose.

Watch out!

You won't gain marks
for adding more than 2
answers for this question.

**Read Text 2 in the Source Booklet provided and
answer Questions 4–6.**

Write your answers in the spaces provided.

4 a From lines 10–16, identify **two** things that show that the inhabitants of
the Great Wild Street District are very poor.

(2 marks)

1 ....

2 ....

b Read this extract.

Fourpenny lodging-houses abound in the district, and it is full of other
dwellings which are not half so comfortable even as fourpenny lodging-
houses. Large families may still be found herding together in dark
underground cellars, not fit for pigs to live in, or in stifling garrets. No
matter how many families may be living in a house, the staircase is never
lighted after the miserable glimmer of daylight has disappeared from its
small dirty windows; and it is generally so badly constructed, so broken,
and so narrow and winding towards the top, as to make it both difficult
and dangerous for a stranger to feel his way up at night time.

From this extract, identify **two** things that suggest that the houses in the
Great Wild Street District are uncomfortable places to live.

(2 marks)

1 ....

2 ....

....

5 Read this extract.

A.B. is a scavenger earning 18s. a week. He has a wife and seven children. They live in a miserable back room with an open recess to it. Two of the children sleep in the same bed with their parents; the rest in a heap on the floor of the recess.

One day when I called upon this family to ascertain why the eldest boy had not been at my school on the previous Sunday, I found him in bed and asked what was the matter with him.

'Oh, sir,' replied the mother, 'there's nothing at all the matter with him, he's well enough. But all the same, he can't go out, and when any one knocks at the door, I make him jump into our bed.'

'But why should he not go out if he is well? and why should you make him jump into bed at this time of day?'

'Well, sir, to tell you the truth the fact is, he's got no trousers to wear.'

In the extract the writer tries to demonstrate that the inhabitants of the Great Wild Street District face significant poverty.

Evaluate how successfully this is achieved.

Give **three** reasons for your opinion and use examples from the extract.

(6 marks)

Time

Spend about **10–12 minutes** on this question.

Unlocking the question

Make sure you understand the main focus of the question.

Unlocking the question

To 'evaluate' means to decide how successful something is.

Watch out!

Make sure you're evaluating how successfully the writer achieves their aims.

Hint

Make a judgement. Open your answer with a clear evaluative sentence.

Unlocking the question

Decide on the three reasons you will use to support your opinion.

Hint

Use short, focused quotations that back up the point you're making.

LEARN IT!

Clearly show your three reasons by using language such as 'first of all', 'secondly' and 'finally', at the beginning of each paragraph.

Hint

You can make your reasons stronger by adding extra points, with language such as 'in addition' and 'furthermore'.

LEARN IT!

Use language to help you state your opinion, like 'I would argue that...', and 'overall, I think that...'.

LEARN IT!

Use P–E–E paragraphs to structure your answer, with a reason, an example and an explanation.

Hint

Consider the writer's tone in this extract. Think about whether it helps make the extract more persuasive in showing that the inhabitants face significant poverty.

Watch out!

Keep your answer tightly focused on the question.

Unlocking the question

Really think about how persuasive the extract is. Explain, as clearly as you can, how persuasive it is and why.

6 For this question refer to the whole of Text 2.

   'In my view, this text shows how difficult it can be to be poor.'

   Based on your evaluation of the text, how far do you agree with
   this opinion?

   Use examples from the text to support your evaluation.

   (12 marks)

LEARN IT!

Use language to explain
your opinion. Use phrases
such as 'this shows that…',
'for this reason, I believe
that…', and 'therefore…'.

Hint

You can make your
evaluation more
convincing by making an
additional point about the
same example from the
text. Use language like
'in addition', and 'what's
more' to do this.

LEARN IT!

Use P–E–E paragraphs
(point, evidence and explain)
to structure your answer.

Watch out!

Remember, your focus
needs to be on the opinion
given in the question.
Each of your points should
discuss how far you agree
with this opinion.

(answer lines)

Hint

You are free to agree,
partially agree or
disagree with the opinion
in the question. You
should always explain why
you think what you do.

Hint

Choose examples from
the text that clearly
support your opinion. Try
to only use quotations
and other evidence that
are relevant to the point
you want to make.

Hint

Think about the tone
and structure of the
whole extract. Do they
help this text show how
difficult it can be to be
poor? Writing about tone
and structure can be an
effective way of showing
that you're thinking about
the whole extract.

Hint

You can write about
structure to discuss how
the writer introduces and
develops their points.
You should then evaluate
how effective this makes
the text.

Time

You should spend about **45 minutes** on this section.

Unlocking the question

You have to answer **one** question – choose **either** Question 7 **or** Question 8.

Hint

Think about the task and your audience. Adapt the content, language and tone of your answer to interest and engage them.

Unlocking the question

For Question 7, you need to continue the answer from the opening paragraph given on the exam paper. This paragraph will give you an idea about what you can write next.

Unlocking the question

Question 8 will give you a list of three topics to cover in your answer. You should write about all three.

Unlocking the question

You need to use accurate spelling, punctuation and grammar for both questions.

SECTION B

Writing

Answer ONE question. You should spend about 45 minutes on this section.

Write your answer in the space provided.

EITHER

*7 Write a speech for 16-year-old students with the title 'Why it's important to help those less fortunate than we are'.

A student has started a response to this task.

Volunteering to help those less fortunate than us can be one of the most rewarding experiences of your life. Everyone wants to do something to help, but where do you start? I would suggest helping someone close to home.

Continue this speech using your own ideas (do not copy information from Texts 1 and 2).

Your response will be marked for the accurate and appropriate use of vocabulary, spelling, punctuation and grammar.

OR

*8 Write a letter of application to an organisation that works with homeless people in your area, applying for a voluntary position.

You should include:

• why you want to volunteer with homeless people in your area

• what you would like to do for the organisation

• the skills and experience you think you can offer the organisation.

Your response will be marked for the accurate and appropriate use of vocabulary, spelling, punctuation and grammar.

(40 marks)

BEGIN YOUR ANSWER ON PAGE 94

Indicate which question you are answering by marking a cross in the box ☒. If you change your mind, put a line through the box ☒ and then indicate your new question with a cross ☒.

Chosen question number: **Question 7** ☐ **Question 8** ☐

Plan your answer to Section B here:

Write your answer to Section B here:

....

....

....

....

....

....

....

....

....

....

....

....

Hint

Improve the quality of your response by using a wide range of punctuation, different sentence types and ambitious vocabulary.

Hint

For Section B, always begin by making a brief, clear plan to guide your writing. Write your plan in the space provided.

Hint

For Question 7, you have to continue the first paragraph given in the question. This paragraph will always give you an idea that you can then develop further.

Unlocking the question

For Question 8, each of the three bullet points you need to write about will provide you with a big idea for your answer. You can develop that idea by including examples, explanation or using persuasive devices, for example.

Unlocking the question

Think about how you could organise your answer. For Question 8, you might want to begin with a short opening paragraph explaining the purpose of your letter.

Hint

Begin each paragraph with a clear topic sentence that explains what the main idea of the paragraph will be.

LEARN IT!

Use phrases like 'first of all', 'secondly' and 'moreover' to introduce new ideas to your text.

LEARN IT!

Use a range of persuasive devices, like emotive language, hyperbole, facts and statistics in your answer. But make sure they fit with the kind of text you're writing!

LEARN IT!

Phrases like 'furthermore' and 'in addition' can be used to develop an idea.

....

....

....

....

....

....

....

....

....

....

....

....

....

....

....

....

....

....

....

....

....

....

....

Hint

Make your writing stand out by including relevant details like people and places, and personal stories (these can be real or imagined). This will make your writing seem less general and more engaging.

Watch out!

For a formal text, write in a formal tone. You should avoid colloquial language and exclamation marks.

Hint

Vary your sentence length and type. Doing this will make your answer seem more interesting to read. For example, some sentences can be short and punchy, others longer and more descriptive. You can use questions, exclamations and command sentences.

Hint

As you write, try to make your answer seem like the text it's supposed to be. If you're writing a speech it should seem like a speech, with direct address to the audience and exclamations to make it lively and engaging.

TOP TIP

Leave around five minutes at the end to proofread your answer! You will be marked on your spelling, punctuation and grammar.

Hint

Use ambitious vocabulary and a range of different punctuation to make your writing more interesting and colourful. But don't overdo it!

If you need more space for your answers, continue writing on your own
separate pieces of paper.

SECTION A

Reading

You should spend about 1 hour 10 minutes on this section.

Read Text 1 in the Source Booklet provided and answer Questions 1–3.

Write your answers in the spaces provided.

1   Identify **four** difficulties that children from the Ragged School face.

(4 marks)

The answer features a short quotation embedded into the sentence.

Answers are short and to the point.

This answer uses a short paraphrase of the text.

1   They have 'nobody at home to take care of them'.

2   Their parents 'teach them to lie and steal'.

3   Some have 'no home to go to'.

4   Many sleep under arches or on steps outside.

The student does not repeat the same information twice.

Each of the student's answers responds directly to the question.

Alternative answers

Answers to Question 1 could also include:

• Their parents 'beat them if they come home without having stolen something'.

• Some children are 'turned out of doors on a bitterly cold night'.

• They have to face 'pitiless snow-storms and pelting rain'.

• Some of these children live in a home 'you would fear to enter'.

2   In lines 1–13, the writer encourages the reader to feel sympathy for the ragged children.

Evaluate how successfully this is achieved.

Give **three** reasons for your opinion and use examples from lines 1–13.

(6 marks)

Q2: sample answer

In my opinion, this extract successfully shows the reader why they should feel sorry for these children. Firstly, the writer describes the problems these children face at home, with parents who force them to steal, and beat them if they don't. 'How would *you* like to be thus treated?' the writer asks. The idea that these children live in fear of violence makes the reader more grateful that they don't, and successfully encourages them to feel sympathetic.

Secondly, the writer uses phrases such as 'poor children' and 'wicked parents'. The first phrase makes the reader sympathise with the children, and the second makes the reader feel angry towards the parents. As parents are supposed to be loving and kind, the reader will sympathise with the children even more strongly.

Thirdly, the writer asks the reader to imagine what it would be like to be forced out of home on a cold winter night. The writer describes the 'pelting rain' and 'pitiless snow-storms', and tells us that we would 'be sorry even if your dog had to stay out on such a night!' The text successfully encourages the reader to sympathise with the children by showing just how unpleasant the weather conditions could be.

The student opens by clearly stating their opinion, and offering a clear evaluative sentence.

The student 'signposts' their answer, introducing their first reason for their opinion.

The first example from the text is a paraphrase, allowing the student to describe the text succinctly.

As well as paraphrasing, the student includes a short, relevant quotation, embedded in the sentence.

This paragraph follows the P–E–E structure.

The student continues to signpost their answer, using the word 'thirdly'.

The student continues to strengthen their paragraphs with several quotes.

This paragraph also convincingly explains why the examples from the text support the student's opinion.

A very strong answer because...

In this answer the student makes a personal judgement on the text, which they introduce with the phrase 'in my opinion'. In each paragraph, the student critically evaluates the text, and shows how the writer encourages the reader to feel sympathy for the Ragged School children. The quotations from the text are short, embedded in the text, and support the evaluative points that the student makes.

Hint

Look at the notes below, and then read the sample answer that follows.

3 How does the writer use language to interest and inform the reader?

You should include:

- the writer's use of language
- the effect on the reader.

Use examples from the whole text and relevant subject terminology.

(8 marks)

Brief annotated quotations give the student ideas to develop in their answer.

Hint

Look at the sample answer to Question 3 to see how the answer develops the points in these annotations.

Q3: sample answer

Plan:

- 'nipping frost', 'pelting rain' – vividly describe the weather
- 'pitiless snow' – personification
- 'warm, comfortable beds' – description with positive connotations
- Use of the pronoun 'you' throughout – speaks directly to the reader; encourages reader to imagine themselves in the Ragged School children's shoes.

A topic sentence makes it clear what the answer will be about.

The student uses short, relevant quotations.

The student specifies the word class.

This answer explores in detail the effect of the writer's language.

The student explores the connotations of individual words.

This paragraph explains the effect of the language on what the reader thinks and feels.

The writer uses language to help the reader vividly imagine the hardships the Ragged School children face. The writer encourages us to imagine being turned out of doors on a 'bitterly cold night', with the 'nipping frost', 'pitiless snow-storms' and 'pelting rain'. The adjectives 'nipping' and 'pelting' emphasise how unpleasant the cold and rain would be, and the personification of the snow storms as 'pitiless' makes them seem even more cruel and harsh. As a result, the reader more clearly imagines some of the struggles these children face.

The writer also contrasts the secure, comfortable life most people enjoy with the difficult lives of these poor children. We are asked to imagine 'nice, warm, comfortable beds', 'plenty of good food', and how nice it is to sleep in 'peace and comfort'. All of these words, like 'warm', 'comfort' and 'peace', have only positive connotations, especially when compared to the 'nipping frost' and 'pelting rain'. The readers can understand even more clearly the difference between their lives and those of these children, and feel even greater sympathy.

Throughout the text, the writer uses the pronoun 'you' to appeal directly to the reader, for example stating 'You would, I hope, be sorry if even your dog had to stay out on such a night!' The use of the pronoun 'you' is effective because it makes the text more personal and impactful than if the Ragged School children were described more distantly. Also, the rhetorical question 'How would you like to be thus treated?' encourages the reader to put themselves in the Ragged School children's shoes and really try to imagine the suffering they have to face. The overall impact is that the text becomes more interesting and engaging to the reader, who is more likely to sympathise with the Ragged School children as a result.

This answer continues to use relevant subject terminology.

The student continues to discuss the impact of the text's language, and how it is used to interest and inform the reader.

Read Text 2 in the Source Booklet provided and
answer Questions 4–6.

Write your answers in the spaces provided.

4   a   From lines 10–16, identify **two** things that show that the inhabitants of
the Great Wild Street District are very poor.

(2 marks)

The quotation is short
and embedded into
the sentence.

Both answers
directly respond to
the question.

1   There are people 'without visible means of living'.
2   Some people find it hard to get enough bread.

**Alternative
answers**

Answers to Question 4a could also include:

• There are 'artisans who are always out of work'.

• Some people find it hard to pay the weekly rent.

• There are 'the poorest of the poor – costermongers'.

• There are 'dealers in rags and bones'.

4 b Read this extract.

From this extract, identify **two** things that suggest that the houses in the Great Wild Street District are uncomfortable places to live.

(2 marks)

Hint

The full extract is not repeated here. Read it on page 87.

1 The attic rooms are 'stifling'.
2 Large families live 'in dark underground cellars'.

Both of these answers respond directly to the question.

Alternative answers

Answers to Question 4b could also include:

• The accommodation isn't 'fit for pigs'.

• There is no lighting on the stairs after daylight disappears.

Hint

The full extract is not repeated here. Read it on page 88.

Hint

Read the notes below, and then look at the sample answer that follows.

5 Read this extract.

In the extract the writer tries to demonstrate that the inhabitants of the Great Wild Street District face significant poverty.

Evaluate how successfully this is achieved.

Give **three** reasons for your opinion and use examples from the extract.

(6 marks)

Writing a good answer

Strong answers to Question 5 will:

• offer a persuasive evaluation on how well the writer has achieved their aims in the extract
• give a personal opinion, using language such as 'in my opinion...' and 'I would argue that...'
• use clear and relevant examples from the text to support the evaluation
• explain how each example from the text supports your opinion.

The opening topic sentence focuses the answer on the question.

The student moves through the extract systematically, making their answer easier to follow.

The student refers to a persuasive device – the list of facts.

The explanation is tightly focused on the question – how effectively the writer shows that these people live in significant poverty.

Q5: sample answer

In this extract, the writer is successful in giving a clear description of poverty in the Great Wild Street District. The extract opens with a list of facts that explain the living conditions of one of the district's families. They have several children and very little space, so little that most of the children must sleep 'in a heap on the floor'. Their home also has an 'open recess' that is not completely protected from the weather. This list of facts makes clear to the reader how unpleasant the living conditions in this district are, and how poor this family must be.

This extract is made even more effective through its serious, dispassionate tone. The writer describes the family's situation through a series of factual statements, with relatively little description or emotion: for example, the opening line simply says that the man 'is a scavenger earning 18s. a week'. In my opinion, this makes the text more trustworthy. The reader feels that the writer is not trying to get them to respond emotionally, but simply to describe the district as it is. The reader will feel confident that they have been given a clear and accurate picture of life in the Great Wild Street District.

Next, the writer tells an anecdote that memorably communicates the reality of the living conditions in this district. He describes visiting the home of one of his pupils, to be told that this pupil cannot leave the house because 'he's got no trousers to wear'. This anecdote communicates to the reader that this family lack even basic necessities, like clothing. The idea of the boy staying inside because he has no trousers is also funny and memorable, and would stay with the reader longer than just a list of facts would.

This topic sentence clearly introduces the subject of this paragraph.

The student makes a point about the writer's tone.

The student continues to give their own, developed opinion on the text.

The student is able to persuasively discuss the impact of the writing.

The student adds layers to their answer by making more than one point about the same piece of evidence.

A very strong answer because...

This answer critically evaluates how well the text demonstrates that the inhabitants of the Great Wild Street District face significant poverty. For example, the student discusses the text's use of facts, and evaluates how effectively they convince the reader. Furthermore, this answer pays close attention to the text's tone, distinguishing between an 'emotive tone' and a 'factual tone', and discussing how this helps the writer achieve their aims. Finally, the answer remains tightly focused on the question, making sensible, well-supported points about how the text manages to persuade the reader.

Hint

Look at the notes given below. Then read the sample answer on the next page.

6   For this question refer to the whole of Text 2.

'In my view, this text shows how difficult it can be to be poor.'

Based on your evaluation of the text, how far do you agree with this opinion?

Use examples from the text to support your evaluation.

(12 marks)

This plan is succinct and outlines the structure for each paragraph.

The answer opens with a clear evaluative sentence, stating the student's opinion.

The opening sentence gives an overview of the major points in the text.

This paragraph is clearly signposted.

The student gives a clear topic sentence explaining the content of the paragraph.

The student skilfully supports their point with a paraphrase of the text.

The paragraph features a clear explanatory sentence.

The quotations are well chosen, and embedded into the sentence.

The student adds a further point to this paragraph to strengthen it.

Use of subject terminology is not required for Question 6, but it can be used to support your evaluation. Here, the student shows how hyperbole contributes to conveying the unpleasantness of living in these houses.

The student links the paragraph back to their evaluation of how successful the text is.

Q6: sample answer

Plan:
- Opening sentence – strongly agree.
- Serious tone, facts, e.g. about the houses and jobs.
- Effect – makes the text seem trustworthy.
- Detailed description of houses – 'stifling garrets', families 'herding together'.
- 'not fit for pigs' – conveys how unpleasant some of the houses are.
- Description of inhabitants' jobs – 'scavengers', 'dealers in rags and bones', 'migratory people'.
- Women 'earn a living in all sorts of ways' – implies prostitution.

I strongly agree that this text demonstrates how hard life can be for the poor, when they don't have even basic necessities such as bread, safe housing and clothing.

First of all, the writer presents his findings in a serious, reserved tone and supports his opinion with numerous facts. He gives the reader facts about the houses in the Great Wild Street District, about the jobs done by the people who live there, and about how they live on a day-to-day basis. By contrast, the writer uses relatively little emotive language. The effect is that the text seems to the reader reliable and accurate, and the reader is therefore more likely to take on board the writer's explanation of how difficult life can be for the poor in the District.

When describing the 'fourpenny lodging-houses' of the district, the writer makes it very clear how difficult it must be to live in houses like these. The houses are clearly not suitable for people to live in: they are 'stifling garrets', with broken and dangerous staircases, where large families 'herd together'. To convey even more forcefully how difficult it must be to live in these houses, the writer uses hyperbole, telling the reader that some of the houses are 'not fit for pigs to live in'. The effect of this is that, as well as receiving an accurate, factual impression of life in these houses, the reader is also given a strong, forceful impression of how unpleasant living there must be.

The writer also gives detailed information about the different jobs done by the inhabitants of the Great Wild Street District, and further informs the reader of the difficulties of being poor. Some of the jobs that these people do include 'scavengers' and 'dealers in rags and bones'. The reader understands the implication that these people will probably earn very little money, and that people without any source of income will find it very hard to survive. We are also told that there are 'women and girls who earn a poor living in all sorts of ways'. This phrase implies that these women must turn to prostitution to survive, further emphasising the difficulties these women face daily.

The student makes a convincing point about the implicit meaning of the language.

For these reasons – the writer's factual tone, his description of the houses of the Great Wild Street District, and of the different jobs done by the inhabitants – in my opinion this text clearly shows how difficult it can be to be poor.

The final paragraph offers a summary of the points made in the answer, and reminds the reader of the student's evaluation.

A very strong answer because...

This answer is well organised, with the first main paragraph looking at the text as a whole, before focusing on different parts of the text. The answer also provides a sustained critical evaluation of the text, considering the factual tone, the description of the 'fourpenny lodging-houses', and of the jobs people in the district do. The student uses phrases like 'the effect of this is' to evaluate the impact of the text on the reader, and how well the writer convinces the reader of their viewpoint. Finally, in this answer the student uses language such as 'I strongly agree' and 'in my opinion' to give a convincing personal opinion, consistently supported by the critical evaluation of the text.

*7 Write a speech for 16-year-old students with the title 'Why it's important to help those less fortunate than we are'.

A student has started a response to this task.

Volunteering to help those less fortunate than us can be one of the most rewarding experiences of your life. Everyone wants to do something to help, but where do you start? I would suggest helping someone close to home.

Continue this speech using your own ideas (do not copy information from Texts 1 and 2).

*Your response will be marked for the accurate and appropriate use of vocabulary, spelling, punctuation and grammar.

(40 marks)

Q7: sample answer

Plan:

Paragraph 1
  Help someone close to home.
  E.g. single parent, elderly person?
You might get something from them too.

Paragraph 2
  Local charity/organisation.
  E.g. homeless people, soup kitchen, litter picking.
  Personal detail – volunteering at a youth club.

Paragraph 3
  Volunteer abroad.
  E.g. teaching, looking after wildlife.
  'Travel broadens the mind'.

Final paragraph – call to action
  Volunteering – one of the most rewarding things you can do with your time.

This plan is simple and to the point. It gives the student an outline to follow when they write the speech.

The student has thought about how they will develop each paragraph.

The student is also thinking about the genre of text they have to write – a speech – and the persuasive techniques that would fit this type of text.

This could be a single parent who needs help, or a kid struggling with homework, or perhaps a lonely elderly person who just wants a chat. Giving someone like this your time and support won't cost you much – in fact, it could be only a few hours a week. Not only that, you might get a lot back yourself! Perhaps the lonely elderly person bakes the most scrumptious cookies! By helping someone who lives close to you, you'll also be making your neighbourhood seem warmer and closer. Who doesn't want that?

Another way you can help is by volunteering for a local charity. From soup kitchens to homeless charities, from litter-picking to taking care of wildlife, there are dozens and dozens of opportunities to help out. Personally, I spend my Saturday mornings volunteering at a local youth club, and I can tell you it's a highlight of my week! If you decide to give your time volunteering, you might well find that the person you really help is you!

Another way you could help – and this one requires more commitment – is to volunteer abroad. In many countries you'll find opportunities to build houses, or teach in schools, or help look after endangered species. Some of our college's recent students went on to do gap years after they finished school, and the blogs they write are amazing! One ex-student volunteered cleaning litter from a beach in Australia... and got to swim with real turtles! I also read about an amazing charity that works with orphaned street children around the world, finding them a loving home and an education. They say that travel broadens the mind, and by volunteering in some exotic locale, you'll get the best of both worlds. What could be better?

So, the next time you're wondering how to spend your weekend, or you feel like 'giving back', consider helping someone who needs it. It will be one of the most rewarding things you can do with your time.

You don't need to copy out the response starter from the question. This student continues writing from the end of those starting sentences.

The examples of different people who might need help make this speech less generalised and more interesting.

The student uses less common vocabulary, like 'scrumptious', that still fits with the tone of the speech.

The ideas in this speech are developed. The student explains why it's important to help those less fortunate than us.

A personal detail is a technique you would expect to find in a speech.

The tone of this speech is consistently lively, upbeat and positive. It is appropriate for a teenage audience, and helps make the idea of helping people seem more appealing.

This speech is well 'signposted', with topic sentences introducing the main idea of each paragraph.

The student uses exclamation marks, but doesn't over-use them. They add to the lively, upbeat tone.

The student consistently addresses their audience to make the speech seem warmer and more personal.

The final paragraph is uplifting and inspires the audience to 'take action', having heard the ideas in the speech.

*8 Write a letter of application to an organisation that works with homeless people in your area, applying for a voluntary position.

You should include:

- why you want to volunteer with homeless people in your area
- what you would like to do for the organisation
- the skills and experience you think you can offer the organisation.

Your response will be marked for the accurate and appropriate use of vocabulary, spelling, punctuation and grammar.

(40 marks)

Q8: sample answer

Plan:

Para 1: intro paragraph – I am writing because...

Para 2: why I want to work with the homeless.

Para 3: my skills and experience.

Para 4: what I want to do for the charity.

Para 5: conclusion; look forward to response.

To whom it may concern,

I'm writing to offer my skills, passion and enthusiasm for working with homeless people in our town. I believe I could be a valuable asset to your organisation.

Let me first give you some information about myself. I'm seventeen, about to enter my final year of college, and I'm passionate about helping people escape poverty and become able to support themselves. At university, I hope to study to be a social worker. I want to gain experience working with some of the most vulnerable people in our community – the homeless. Furthermore, I believe that homelessness is one of the most significant problems we face today. We live in a prosperous, developed country, and yet there are still some people who have no place to stay. Why aren't we trying to solve this problem? How can we help people get off the streets? I'm fascinated by these questions, and plan on dedicating my career to answering them.

I have a number of skills that I think make me an ideal candidate for this kind of work. I'm a good listener, and listen attentively and compassionately as people talk about their struggles and the pain they've experienced. In addition, I'm good at building friendships with people, by remembering things about them and gaining their trust. This, I believe, would help me to foster strong connections with some of the vulnerable people you work with. Also, for the last two years I've been working as a mentor to younger students at my college, so I've developed useful experience working with people.

This short, concise plan shows how the student will cover all three bullet points in the question.

This introductory paragraph makes the purpose of the letter clear.

The language of this letter is more formal. The student does not use exclamation marks, or colloquial (informal) language. The style is appropriate to the genre and audience.

Even though this is a formal letter, the student makes their letter more personal and engaging.

These rhetorical questions are persuasive, and reveal the student's passion for the subject.

Each paragraph begins with a clear topic sentence.

Phrases like 'furthermore' and 'in addition' are used to develop the ideas.

This letter is well structured, beginning by explaining why the student wants to volunteer with the homeless, before moving on to the skills they could offer, and what they would like to do for the organisation. The student makes sure they address each bullet point in the question.

Ideally, I'd like to volunteer by working on the frontline talking to homeless people directly or doing practical tasks like serving in the soup kitchen. Please don't put me somewhere in an office, filling out forms and replying to emails — that really wouldn't match with my skillset or interests. Or perhaps, if you have a position that involves going out into the street to work with people, you would consider me for that too. I'm always open to broadening my horizons and trying out new things.

I hope this letter makes clear my enthusiasm for working with your organisation, and demonstrates my suitability as a candidate. I'm happy to provide you with any more information if you need it, and I look forward to your response.

Yours faithfully,

The final paragraph of this answer repeats the student's interest in working for the charity. It makes the letter seem more persuasive.

The student starts and ends their letter with the correct phrases.

A very strong answer because...

This letter follows a clear, logical structure, as the student first gives the reason why they're writing, then discusses why they want to work with the homeless, before explaining how they could help the organisation. Each paragraph has one main idea, and this is made clear through the opening topic sentence. The tone is formal, though there are also plenty of details about the applicant's life that make the letter seem more personal. Above all, it **sounds** like a letter someone would write to apply for a job or voluntary position.

Understanding Question 1

Question 1 will always be the same. It will ask you to identify one piece of explicit information from the text. It's worth one mark.

How does Question 1 work?

This question tests your ability to pick out information from a text.

Look out for the line numbers – this is where you will find the information you need to answer the question.

This question will always ask you to 'identify'.

'One' tells you that you only need to find one piece of information.

> From lines 1–6, identify **one** way Gatsby and his staff prepare for parties.
>
> **(1 mark)**

In your Paper 2 exam, Text 1 will be in your Source Booklet. For this example, you can find the relevant extract below.

Text 1, lines 1–6

There was music from my neighbor's house through the summer nights. On week-ends his Rolls-Royce became an omnibus, bearing parties to and from the city, between nine in the morning and long past midnight, while his station wagon scampered like a brisk yellow bug to meet all trains. And on Mondays eight servants including an extra gardener toiled all day with mops and scrubbing-brushes and hammers and garden-shears, repairing the ravages of the night before.

What does Question 1 assess?

☑ Question 1 tests Assessment Objective 1.

☑ You need to show your ability to pick out explicit information from the text.

See page 7 to read about explicit information.

How long should I spend?

Spend 1–2 minutes on Question 1.

Try not to spend longer than a minute or two as the questions that follow need more time.

How is Question 1 marked?

You need to correctly pick out one detail that relates to the question.

☑ There is one mark available for this question so you only need to provide one piece of information.

☑ Adding extra information will **not** improve your answer.

What does 'identify' mean?

To identify means to spot or pick something out. You need to answer the question exactly, so pay close attention to what you are being asked to find.

TOP TIP

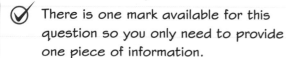

Make sure you pick one piece of information from the lines specified – check the line numbers.

Answering Question 1

Question 1 should be a chance for you to answer a straightforward question at the beginning of your exam paper.

Reading the question

From lines 1–6, identify **one** way Gatsby and his staff prepare for parties.

(1 mark)

Always read the question carefully before you start writing your answer. Make sure you are clear about what the question is asking you to do. In this case, you need to find **one** piece of information that tells the reader how Gatsby prepares for parties.

Steps to success

1 Read the question carefully.

2 Select **one** piece of information from the extract that answers the question.

There will be more than one piece of relevant information, so it's important to choose one that you feel answers the question directly.

3 Write the answer in the space provided – you don't have to write in full sentences.

You can choose to quote directly from the text, or write the answer in your own words (paraphrase).

Getting it right

Remember, you only need to identify **one** piece of information. Here are some examples of answers you could give.

Gatsby's Rolls-Royce is sent to bring people to and from the city.

✓ This answer gives a brief description of one piece of information from the text.

servants including an extra gardener toiled all day with mops and scrubbing-brushes and hammers and garden-shears

✗ This answer gives more information than is necessary. The student could be more specific to save time.

The servants cleaned the house with mops.

✓ This answer gives enough information.

✗ This information is not available in the lines given in the question.

The servants made food for the party.

Understanding Question 2

Question 2 will always be structured in the same way. It will ask you to read a short extract from Text 1, and then analyse the language used.

How does Question 2 work?

> 2   Read this extract.
>
> > The bar is in full swing and floating rounds of cocktails permeate the garden outside until the air is alive with chatter and laughter and casual innuendo and introductions forgotten on the spot and enthusiastic meetings between women who never knew each other's names.
>
> In the extract, **how** does the writer use language to create a sense of the atmosphere at the party?
>
> Use examples from the extract and relevant subject terminology.
>
> **(6 marks)**

You will always be provided with an extract to read. Your answer should be based on this extract only.

You will be asked to explain **how** language has been used. This means explaining the effect of the language features that you choose.

Here is the topic of the question – make sure you select language features that relate only to this topic.

This means you should quote from the text in your answer.

Use 'relevant subject terminology' to improve the quality of your response.

The question is worth six marks.

What does Question 2 assess?

☑ Question 2 tests Assessment Objective 2.

☑ You need to show your ability to **analyse** the language a writer has used.

☑ You should use relevant subject terminology.

How long should I spend?

You should spend 8–10 minutes answering Question 2.

You need time to select suitable points and explain them.

For more information on using subject terminology, see page 13.

What does 'analyse' mean?

To analyse means to consider the reasons why something is the way it is – in this case, why a writer has chosen specific words or phrases in order to make the reader picture a scene, or feel a certain way.

TOP TIP

Analysing language begins with looking at the words and phrases that the writer has chosen. Pick a word that stands out and try to work out what the writer wants the reader to imagine when they read that word.

TOP TIP

When you read the extract, try to imagine the scene in your head. How does it make you feel? Why do you think it makes you feel that way? Which words or phrases cause those feelings?

Understanding Question 2

Analysing language

Your answer should offer ways in which the writer has used language to present something specific in the text. You will need to use evidence from the text to explain how these examples affect the reader.

How does the writer use language to create a sense of atmosphere?

The writer talks about all the sounds he can hear at the party.

This is a valid example of a way in which the writer uses language to create a sense of the atmosphere at the party.

Support your point using a direct reference to the text.

Details in the text that tell me this:

'the air is alive with chatter and laughter and casual innuendo'

The supporting detail can quote or paraphrase words from the text, or be a valid comment about it.

Relevant subject terminology:

the repetition of the word 'and' shows the reader how busy it is.

The use of the word 'repetition' is an example of relevant subject terminology.

See page 16 for more about creating atmosphere, and page 40 for more on using the senses in writing.

How is Question 2 marked?

High-quality answers will offer examples of how the writer has used language to achieve a particular effect.

✓ Analyse the text and how language is used.

✓ Support your points with evidence from the text.

✓ Use relevant subject terminology to explain how the writer's language is effective.

For more on subject terminology, refer to pages 13–14.

Relevant subject terminology

There are many examples of subject terminology you could identify and use for your answer to Question 2. Here are some to look out for:

- word classes – verbs, adjectives, nouns or adverbs
- sound effects such as alliteration and onomatopoeia
- sensory language – anything that helps the reader to imagine what the writer can see, smell, taste, hear or feel
- imagery – similes, metaphors, personification
- repetition of words or phrases.

TOP TIP

Top tips for success

✓ Revise subject terminology regularly to make sure you're able to use it confidently to name language features in your exam.

✓ Make sure that you know what the **effect** of the language feature is rather than just naming it correctly.

✓ Read the extract carefully and search for your answers from within it.

✓ Pick out details that you feel comfortable explaining – if you don't know the meaning of a word, don't use it.

Answering Question 2

Question 2 will always ask you to analyse the language in an extract.

Reading the question

In the extract, how does the writer use language to create a sense of the atmosphere at the party?

Use examples from the extract and relevant subject terminology.

(6 marks)

Always read the question carefully to find out what you need to do.

The question is worth six marks so you will need to develop your answers and write in full sentences.

Refer to page 115 for the extract you have to read for this example question.

Steps to success

1 Read the extract carefully, looking out for language features and devices.

2 Make one valid point about a language feature in the extract and support it using an example from the text.

The writer uses the word 'and' to give the impression that there is lots going on. The writer says 'the air is alive with chatter and laughter and casual innuendo' to describe the sounds he can hear at the party.

Write one sentence to introduce your idea.

Your example could be a direct quotation, or you can explain in your own words. Don't rewrite large chunks of the extract.

3 Add an extra sentence using relevant subject terminology.

The <u>repetition</u> of the word 'and' suggests there is so much going on that the writer is struggling to take it all in.

Revise subject terminology to give yourself the best chance of naming various language features in the extracts.

This correctly identifies the language feature and explains how it gives a sense of the atmosphere at the party.

4 Improve your answer by making another point about the same quotation.

Furthermore, the word '<u>chatter</u>' is an example of <u>onomatopoeia</u>. This helps the reader to imagine the sounds the writer can hear, and gives a sense of the atmosphere at the party.

Pay particular attention to quotations to explain the effects of specific words or short phrases.

TOP TIP

Keep track of time, and the number of points you've made, to make sure you don't spend too much time on Question 2.

Answering Question 2

Getting it right

Use short quotations and make the most of your knowledge of language techniques to write a good response to Question 2 without taking too long over it. Re-read Question 2 on page 117 and look at these student responses.

The writer makes the people at the party sound as though they aren't very interested in each other. He describes 'meetings between enthusiastic women that never knew each other's names'.

✗ The question asks about the atmosphere at the party, not about the types of people there.

✗ The point might be correct but it doesn't relate to the topic of the question.

✗ The evidence does support the point, but it is not related to the topic of the question.

The writer makes the atmosphere at the party sound magical and lively and really noisy. He writes 'The bar is in full swing and floating rounds of cocktails permeate the garden outside until the air is alive with chatter and laughter and casual innuendo'.

✓ This answer directly addresses the topic of the question.

✗ This is too much information. The student could make three separate points here, backed up by different pieces of evidence. Focus each sentence on one specific point.

✗ There is no need to copy out large portions of the extract – this does not show the student's ability to give evidence for their point, plus it takes a long time.

✗ The answer doesn't contain any subject terminology.

The writer creates a sense of atmosphere by describing the sounds he can hear at the party. He says 'the air is alive with chatter and laughter'. The use of the onomatopoeic word 'chatter' really brings the description of the party to life, and the use of sensory language helps the reader to imagine they are there.

✓ This shows **how** the writer has created a sense of atmosphere.

✓ A short, focused quotation is quick to write and relates directly to the point just made.

✓ Naming the subject terminology you recognise **and** explaining its effect is an example of a high-level answer.

✓ Extend your point by making a further comment about the quotation, also using another subject-specific term, to improve the quality of your answer.

Understanding Question 3

Question 3 will always be the same. It refers to Text 2 and will ask you to identify one thing from an extract.

How does Question 3 work?

Like Question 1, Question 3 tests your ability to pick out information from a text. However, for Question 3 you will need to read between the lines to pick out the implicit information.

Read this extract.

> Culinary choices are only the start of the potential tensions on board. Compared with the five-star hotel standard of the guest state-rooms, the crew accommodation is usually cramped and shared. Crew will wake up to serve breakfast and then stay until the last guest has gone to bed, meaning days can be up to 20 hours. There are no weekends at sea. On superyachts the owner is God, followed quickly by the captain and the guests.

From the extract, identify **one** thing that shows life is hard work for the crew of the superyachts.

(1 mark)

Just like Question 1, Question 3 will always ask you to 'identify' information.

'One' tells you that you only need to find one piece of implicit information.

For Question 3, you will always be given a short extract from the text.

Question 3 is worth one mark.

To find out more about implicit information, see pages 8 and 10.

The question topic

The question topic is the subject which you are being asked about.

> From the extract, identify **one** thing that shows <u>life is hard work for the crew of the superyachts.</u>

The topic of this question is how life is hard work for the crew.

What does Question 3 assess?

☑ Question 3 tests Assessment Objective 1.

☑ You need to show your ability to pick out implicit information from the text.

How long should I spend?

Spend 1–2 minutes on Question 3.

Try not to spend longer than a minute or two as the following questions will require more time.

How is Question 3 marked?

Only one mark is available, so you need to correctly pick out one piece of information that relates to the question.

☑ There is one mark available for Question 3 so you need to provide only one answer.

☑ Remember, adding extra information does not improve your answer.

How much should I write?

There will always be more than one possible answer, but that doesn't mean you need to write more or explain your answer.

TOP TIP

You don't need to explain **how** a writer has shown something for Question 3 – it's enough to just to pick out a single piece of information.

Answering Question 3

Question 3 is another opportunity to answer a fairly straightforward question. Stay tightly focused on the topic and don't spend too long over it.

Locating relevant information

Look at what the question is asking you to do:

> From the extract, identify **one** thing that shows life is hard work for the crew of the superyachts.

The question topic is 'life is hard work for the crew of the superyachts'. As you read the extract in the question on page 119, focus on the topic and try to match it to words and phrases within the text. For example, the topic is 'hard work' so you might underline the words '20 hours'.

Steps to success

1 Read the question carefully.

2 Find **one** piece of information in the extract that addresses the topic of the question.

3 Write the answer in the space provided – you don't have to write in full sentences.

You can either quote directly from the text or you can write the answer in your own words.

Getting it right

Remember, you only need to identify **one** piece of implicit information. You will need to look at the text carefully to identify what the writer is implying.

The crew have to share rooms and don't have any privacy.
 ✗ This answer refers to the crew's living conditions rather than their work.

Crew will wake up to serve breakfast.
 ✗ This answer does talk about the work, but it doesn't suggest it's hard.

The crew aren't allowed to go to bed until after the last guest.
 ✓ This suggests how the work is hard for the crew.

The crew have to work very long days.
 ✓ The information given is concise and is paraphrased from the text.

'There are no weekends at sea.'
 ✓ This suggests the crew have no time to relax – but you don't need to explain this as the question did not ask you **how** the writer shows it's hard work for the crew.

Understanding Question 4

Question 4 will ask you to use the whole of Text 2 to explain how the writer tries to interest and engage the reader. You will need to refer to both language and structure in this question.

How does Question 4 work?

This question tests your knowledge of how language and structure are used to interest and engage readers. It refers to Text 2.

> The writer presents life aboard superyachts.
>
> How does the writer try to interest and engage the reader?
>
> You should include:
> - the writer's use of language
> - the writer's use of structure
> - the effect on the reader.
>
> Use examples from the whole text and relevant subject terminology.
>
> **(10 marks)**

Begin by reading the topic of the question. In this case it is 'life aboard superyachts.'

You should consider the words, phrases, techniques and quotations the writer has chosen. You need to analyse structure – punctuation, sentence lengths and types, paragraphs and how the writer has organised the subjects in the text.

You will need to write about how these elements are interesting to the reader.

'Use examples' means you should quote from the text in your answer.

Question 4 is worth ten marks.

Use subject terminology to support your points, in order to improve the quality of your answer.

How long should I spend?

You should spend 12–15 minutes answering Question 4. Give yourself time to develop your points.

What does Question 4 assess?

- ✓ Question 4 tests Assessment Objective 2.
- ✓ You need to write about the effects that a writer's use of language and structure has on a reader.
- ✓ Improve your answer by using relevant subject terminology to support your points.

What has an 'effect on the reader'?

Writers use certain language devices and structural elements to try to make the reader interested in what they have to say.

Writers may use language devices and varied vocabulary to help emphasise their ideas. Structure – the way a piece is organised and laid out on the page – can help to keep a reader engaged.

For more about beginnings and endings, go to page 42. For more on different types of sentence, see page 49.

TOP TIP

When you're reading, be aware of words, phrases or devices that stand out. Consider what it is about them that caught your attention.

TOP TIP

When you read, try to work out why the writer began and ended the way they did. If they have used any short sentences, or single-sentence paragraphs, think about why they might have done that.

Understanding Question 4

Analysing language and structure

In your answer, you need to give examples of **both** language and structure. You will not write a good answer if you talk about only language or only structure.

How does the writer use language and structure to interest and engage the reader?

The writer interests the reader by using paragraphs to shape the text. Firstly the writer introduces ideas about the luxury of the superyachts, and then contrasts that with what life is like for the staff who work on board.

This is a detail about the **structure** of the piece. Each paragraph introduces a new idea which would interest and engage the reader. In this answer, the word 'paragraph' is an example of **relevant subject terminology**.

Use examples from the text to support the point.

The writer begins by describing the yachts from the outside, moves on to outline the work the staff do on board, and then talks about what conditions are like for the crew.

Often, when talking about overall structure, it's easier to paraphrase – to put an idea in your own words – than to quote directly. Copying long quotations would take too long and would not improve your answer.

Include points on both language and structure.

The writer engages the reader by making them feel sympathetic towards the staff. Crew members have to clean 'constantly', and life for them can be 'horrific'.

You can improve your answer by considering the effect of word choices. For example, the writer has used the word 'horrific' to describe the life on board for the staff. The use of this strong adjective would have an effect on the reader – it would evoke sympathy for the workers having to endure such unpleasant working conditions.

How is Question 4 marked?

High-quality answers to Question 4:

- ✓ give examples of how language and structure are used to interest or engage the reader
- ✓ support points with evidence
- ✓ use relevant subject terminology to successfully support their explanations.

See the bottom of page 124 for top tips on answering Question 4.

Relevant subject terminology – structure

Here are some examples of terminology you can use to talk about structure:

- paragraphs
- sentence length and type
- repetition
- lists
- dialogue
- punctuation
- changing of tense
- unusual word order (e.g. starting a sentence with a verb)
- order of events
- order of ideas or feelings.

Answering Question 4

Question 4 will always ask you to look at the whole of an extract, and to consider both language and structure. Make sure you are thorough and include examples of each in your answer.

Reading the question

The writer presents a description about life aboard superyachts.

How does the writer try to interest and engage the reader?

You should include:

- the writer's use of language
- the writer's use of structure
- the effect on the reader.

Use examples from the whole text and relevant subject terminology.

(10 marks)

Read the question carefully to find out what you need to do.

Make at least one point about language.

Make at least one point about structure.

For all the points you make, try to explain how the example you have chosen has an effect on the reader.

The question is worth ten marks so you will need to write a detailed response.

You need to pick specific examples from the text to support your points, and continue to use subject-specific terminology.

Steps to success

❶ Read the extract carefully and make your first point on language or structure.

The writer contrasts the luxury of the superyacht with how hard life is for the staff on board. The writer says, 'Compared with the five-star hotel standard of the guest state-rooms, the crew accommodation is usually cramped and shared'. The first clause in the sentence describes the high quality of the accommodation for the guests, and the second provides a direct contrast.

State your first point.

Use a direct quotation, or explain in your own words.

Refer to just the part that supports your point – don't rewrite large chunks of text.

❷ Explain the effect your example has on the reader.

This contrast helps the reader to imagine how much harder it must be for the staff, as they see the guests living in luxury while they are uncomfortable and have very little space.

Use the P–E–E paragraph structure – 'Point–Evidence–Explain' – to stay focused on your points.

❸ Extend your answer.

The writer's use of the adjective 'cramped' helps the reader to understand how uncomfortable the crew's living space is.

Focus on words or short phrases and explain their effect in context.

Name the specific word class if you can. Only do this if you feel confident; if not, move on to your next point.

Next, move on to your next point, repeating steps 1–4.

Answering Question 4

Getting it right

Using what you have noticed about language and structure, develop your answer with short quotations and subject terminology to succeed on Question 4. Re-read the question on page 123 and look at these student answers.

✔ Writing about the use of paragraphs is a valid point about the structure of a text.

> The writer uses several different paragraphs to introduce different ideas about life aboard the superyachts.
>
> The writer talks about the jobs the staff do on board, and how it isn't very much fun.

✘ The point is correct but it doesn't address the question fully. The answer needs to explain why introducing different ideas about life aboard the superyachts might interest and engage the reader.

✘ The evidence does not really support the point that has been made, nor does it answer the question of how the writer interests and engages the reader.

✔ This answer picks out a specific thing from the text, and goes on to explain how it would interest and engage the reader.

> The writer makes life on board the superyachts sound really hard for the staff, but really luxurious for the guests. This contrast would interest the reader as they would be able to identify with one or both points of view. 'The deckhands sent into the ocean to manually clear the area of jellyfish before a guest went swimming.'

✔ The student uses subject-specific terminology here with the word 'contrast'.

✔ The reason **why** the reader would be interested by this specific point is explained clearly.

✘ Although this quotation supports the point, it needs to be connected to it.

✔ This shows **how** the writer has created a sense of atmosphere.

> The writer creates a sense of the atmosphere of luxury and excess by listing the 'ridiculous' things that happen, such as 'dry cleaning sent to Paris'. Repetition of the sentence structure where each of four sentences starts with 'the' plus a noun emphasises that the guests have whole lists of outlandish demands that are catered for, no matter how expensive or difficult: 'Anything and everything procured on demand'.

✔ A short, focused quotation is quick to write and relates directly to the point just made.

✔ Naming the subject terminology you recognise and explaining its effect is an example of a high-level answer.

TOP TIP

Top tips for success

✔ Read the extract again and underline or make notes in the margin when you notice a language or structural feature. Remember you need to talk about both.

✔ Vary your answers – there might be three examples of repetition, but you will produce a better answer if you write about different types of language and structure.

✔ Be aware of your own reactions as you read the texts in the exam.

Understanding Question 5

In Question 5 you will review **both** texts, searching for similarities between the texts and supporting your choices with evidence.

How does Question 5 work?

This question will always give you the connection between the two texts – this is the 'theme' of the texts.

Question 5 is about finding similarities between the texts, not differences.

Text 1 and Text 2 both show experiences of living in a wealthy environment. The circumstances are different, but they share similarities.

Write a summary giving **three** separate ways the experiences of living in a wealthy environment are similar.

Support **each separate similarity** with evidence from **both** texts.

(6 marks)

A summary means you don't need to go into too much detail.

The question asks for three similarities – make sure you find three, but don't add more as this will not improve your answer.

Question 5 is worth six marks.

As in other questions, you need to find evidence from the texts to support your points.

You need to search both texts for similarities and provide a summary of these.

For an explanation of implicit information, see page 8. Page 7 explains explicit information.

How long should I spend?

You should spend about 10 minutes on Question 5. Only six marks are available so don't spend too long over it.

What does Question 5 assess?

- ✓ Question 5 tests Assessment Objective 1.
- ✓ You need to pick out explicit and implicit information from **both** texts for this question.
- ✓ You must try to find three separate ways that the texts are similar.
- ✓ You need to support your points with evidence.

How do I pick out similarities?

Although the two texts given in your exam will be different in many ways, they will always be linked by a **theme**.

Your job in Question 5 is to spot the **connections** between the two texts, and to write about them. Be careful not to choose differences – you can talk about these in Question 6.

TOP TIP

The theme of the texts will always be in the question, so if you're not sure where to start, re-read the question for clues.

TOP TIP

Underline the main ideas presented in one text as you read, and decide whether you think the other text contains a similar idea. If not, make a note as you might be able to talk about it in Question 6.

Understanding Question 5

Finding three similarities

1 **Read the texts and make notes** in the margins when you find similarities. For example, if you spot a detail about dining in one text, note it down. Then if you find a detail about dining in the second text, note that down too. You could even use matching symbols to mark them. This will make it quicker for you to find them when you write your summary.

2 Pick out something that is **common to both texts**, that **relates to the theme** given in the question.

> In both texts, the writers talk about the different jobs the staff perform to prepare for parties and events.

Summarise means be brief and do not go into lots of detail. You have to make three points, and you don't have long.

3 **Support** each separate similarity with **evidence from both texts**.

> In Text 1 the writer talks about how the servants clean and repair damage to the house, and in Text 2 there is mention of cleaning toilets 'with toothbrushes' and sending dry cleaning 'to Paris'.

Short quotations from the text are embedded into the sentences here; this is a quick and tidy way of incorporating relevant evidence.

4 Make sure **each point is different**.

> In both texts, the writers write about the tasks that members of staff perform for their employers' guests.

This is not a good answer as it makes the same point as the previous answer. Try to make sure your points are different from one another. Also, it does not make proper reference to the text.

> For Question 5 you should consider the content, the writer's ideas and the themes presented in the text.

How is Question 5 marked?

You will be awarded marks for finding three similarities between the two texts, summarising them and giving evidence.

- ☑ Answers must provide three similarities to be successful.
- ☑ The points must be distinct – try to find three similarities that are different from one another.
- ☑ High-level answers will successfully support their points with evidence.

Phrases for describing similarities

There are a few words and phrases you can use to start your sentences when comparing two texts.

> Similarly,...
>
> Both texts show...
>
> In both texts,...
>
> Both Text 1 and Text 2...
>
> Firstly,.../Secondly,.../Thirdly,...

Answering Question 5

Question 5 will always ask you to summarise the similarities between both extracts. Make sure you refer to both Text 1 and Text 2.

Reading the question

Text 1 and Text 2 both show experiences of living in a wealthy environment. The circumstances are different, but they share similarities.

Write a summary giving **three** separate ways the experiences of living in a wealthy environment are similar.

Support **each separate similarity** with evidence from **both** texts.

(6 marks)

Always read the question carefully to find out what you need to compare.

The question will always indicate the connection between the texts to help guide you.

A summary means brief, clear sentences, and not too much detail.

Focus your answer only on similarities, not differences.

You need to use examples from the text to support your points.

The question is worth six marks so you will need to write briefly and clearly and not take too long.

Steps to success

1 Read the texts carefully, and look for something relating to living in a wealthy environment that is mentioned in both Text 1 and Text 2.

2 Write your first similarity. Use a brief sentence to explain it.

The first similarity the texts share is that they both talk about the kinds of food that are prepared.

The sentence does not need to go into any detail as your evidence will explain your choice.

3 Support your point using evidence from each text.

In Text 1 the writer talks about the different kinds of food the caterers bring, including 'pastry pigs', and in Text 2 the writer describes how a pig is flown in for a 'hog roast'.

Either use a direct quotation or explain in your own words.

Make sure you refer to **both texts** in your evidence.

4 Move on to your next similarity. Explain it, then give your evidence from the text.

A second similarity is that both texts present the staff that attend to the guests. Text 1 talks about how many different staff are working to prepare for their employer's party guests. Similarly, Text 2 describes how there is a crew on board the superyachts, and the yachts need 'cleaning constantly'.

Do not spend any longer than you need to on each point.

Vary the types of things you write about. For example, don't write three points about food.

Answering Question 5

Getting it right

Find similarities between the two texts, linked to the question topic, and give a summary of them. You do not need to explain how the writers use language or structure in this question. Keep it brief and to the point.

✓ This is a good choice of subject as both texts discuss cleaning.

✗ However, the points made about this similarity are not linked to the focus of the question which is 'living in a wealthy environment'.

✓ This quotation is suitable evidence for the point made about Text 1. It's brief and no explanation is provided; this is all that is required for Question 5.

✗ This is evidence that supports a point about cleaning. However, it doesn't match the point that was made about Text 2. Make sure your evidence matches the point you are making, and that your points for both texts are linked.

> Text 1 talks about the cleaning at the parties and Text 2 talks about the strange things the crew are asked to do. Text 1 talks about 'mops and scrubbing brushes' and Text 2 mentions 'unblocking toilets'.

✗ This point is wrong for both texts. In Text 1, there is no indication of how the staff get along with the party-goers. Similarly, in Text 2 we are not told how well the crew and owners or guests get along, but overall the owners do not seem to treat the crew well.

✗ This example does not link to the point being made.

✗ The evidence here could possibly support the point being made. However, we can infer from the rest of the text that the owners are domineering and expect the crew to obey them. There is no indication of how well or otherwise they get along.

✗ The answer does not link to the question as it does not describe living in a wealthy environment, which is written about in the texts.

> The texts both show the staff and the party-goers get along well. Text 1 shows the orchestra arriving, and in Text 2 the owners of the superyachts are described as 'God'.

✓ This is clearly a similarity as the word 'both' indicates.

✓ This point is clearly expressed in both pieces.

✓ This evidence supports the point.

✓ Both quotations are brief and support the point being made.

> Both Text 1 and Text 2 talk about how hard the staff have to work for their employers. Text 1 says that eight servants 'toiled all day', and Text 2 says 'days can be up to 20 hours' for the crew.

Understanding Question 6

Question 6 will ask you to consider the whole of both texts, and to compare the writers' ideas and the way in which they present their viewpoints on a particular theme.

How does Question 6 work?

'Compare' means to find similarities and differences between two things – in this case, the two exam texts.

You will be given the theme of the texts in the question. This is what you need to focus your answer on.

Compare the writers' ideas and perspectives about the lives of the rich.

You should compare the writers':

- main ideas
- points of view
- presentation of these ideas and views.

Use examples from both texts to support your comparison.

(16 marks)

You will need to work out the main ideas that each text is trying to express, and compare them.

Each text will have a different point of view about the theme. You need to compare these as part of your answer.

You need to find evidence from both texts to support your points.

Question 6 is worth 16 marks.

What does Question 6 assess?

- ✓ Question 6 tests Assessment Objective 3.
- ✓ You need to compare writers' ideas and perspectives and how they are expressed across **two** texts.
- ✓ You need to compare the ideas presented, as well as **how** they are presented.
- ✓ You should support your points with evidence.

How long should I spend?

You should spend about 20 minutes on Question 6. It's worth 16 marks so you need to develop your answer and provide plenty of detail from both texts.

Comparison – differences

Here are some useful words and phrases for comparing texts, particularly when you are pointing out differences.

In Text 1..., **whereas** in Text 2...

On the other hand,...

While Text 1 shows..., Text 2 shows...

The writers have **contrasting** views.

However,...

See page 126 for phrases you can use when describing similarities.

How do I work out the ideas and points of view?

Both of your exam texts will share a theme. However, it is likely that they will approach it from different angles or perspectives, and with different opinions.

Try to work out what impressions of the theme the writer or narrator is trying to convey to the reader.

TOP TIP

Try to identify the methods the two writers use – for example humour, emotive language, exaggeration. Think about how effective they are.

TOP TIP

Think about the tone and mood of the texts – for example, whether they are positive/negative towards the theme.

Understanding Question 6

Comparing texts

To answer Question 6 successfully, you will need to develop points using **both** texts.
You can talk about:

- the themes and ideas the writers present
- the attitudes and points of view of the writers, and
- the language and the structure used to present these ideas.

For more about comparing texts, see pages 21–24.

Identifying and comparing ideas

Identify one of the main ideas presented in one of the texts. Then see how the second text approaches the same idea.

> In Text 1, the writer gives the impression that the rich enjoy life, and the parties held at the house are a lot of fun, whereas in Text 2, the staff who work on the superyachts present life on board more negatively, suggesting the rich yacht owners are demanding and unpleasant.

Compare the ways the writers have presented the ideas. In this example, the two writers' contrasting language clearly shows their point of view:

> In Text 1 the use of nouns such as 'laughter' and adjectives such as 'cheerful' create a positive impression of an enjoyable atmosphere. On the other hand, Text 2 contains less positive language, for example words like 'tensions' and 'excess', which create a negative impression.

Identifying attitudes and points of view

- Look out for strong vocabulary in non-fiction pieces to help you work out a writer's opinion. If they use words like 'terrible' and 'disgusting' they probably have a negative viewpoint on the theme. If they use vocabulary like 'wonderful', they may have a positive viewpoint.
- Writers often appeal to the emotions of their readers to create an effect. Be alert for your own reactions – if you read something that makes you feel sad, guilty or angry, underline it and try to work out which words or phrases create this emotion.
- In fiction, look out for other clues the writer has used to create mood. For example, the writer may use descriptions of the weather. If it's cloudy, stormy or raining this can express an unsettled or negative mood. If the sun is shining, it can create a positive mood.

How is Question 6 marked?

You will need to consider **both texts** in full.

- ✓ You will earn marks for identifying and comparing ideas presented in **both** texts.
- ✓ You need to explain how the ideas and points of view have been presented.
- ✓ You should use evidence from both texts to support your points.

Top tips for success

TOP TIP

- ✓ Develop your points fully.
- ✓ Think 'what, how, why?' – **what** idea the writer is presenting, **how** they are presenting it, and **why** this is effective.
- ✓ Look for points the texts agree on, and points they disagree on.
- ✓ If one text focuses on a different part of the theme than the other, you can talk about that. Explain why the focus is an effective way of expressing the writer's point of view.

Answering Question 6

Question 6 is all about looking at the two texts as a whole. You must support your points with evidence and explain how the writers have tried to present their ideas and perspectives.

Reading the question

You need to think about (i) ideas and (ii) perspectives – this means (i) what the writers are talking about and (ii) how they feel about it, and how they want the reader to feel.

The question will always ask you to consider the theme of the two pieces – even if the texts are very different, they will always be about the same topic.

Compare the writers' ideas and perspectives about the lives of the rich.

You should compare the writers':

- main ideas
- points of view
- presentation of these ideas and views.

Use examples from both texts to support your comparison.

(16 marks)

You need to consider both texts throughout your answer.

Compare the language used by the writers, the way the texts are structured, and the way the writers interact with the theme.

Not only do you need to use examples from both texts, in Question 6 you also need to link your examples, and say how they are similar, or different.

Steps to success

1 Review the two texts and pick out one of the main ideas or perspectives that one of the two texts is presenting. Write it out, referring to both texts.

Text 1 presents a positive impression of the lives of the rich, whereas Text 2 presents a more negative impression.

Make a point that compares an idea or perspective across both texts.

Use comparative language (e.g. 'whereas') to explain differences.

2 Give evidence from both texts to support your point.

In Text 1 the writer uses adjectives such as 'joyous', 'cheerful' and 'brighter' whereas in Text 2, the yacht owners seem unreachable, living in a world that is 'impossible to touch' and where 'riff-raff' are not welcome.

Use subject-specific terminology when it is relevant.

Remember to include evidence from both texts.

Evidence can be a single word or phrase.

3 Explain how the writers present the idea or perspective you have picked out.

The use of positive vocabulary in Text 1 gives the impression that the writer thinks the rich have exciting, happy lives. In Text 2, the writer creates a contrasting impression by indicating that the rich are concerned only with showing off their wealth and maintaining their position.

Look at the evidence in the texts. Link it to your point to make the connection.

Now compare that with the second text – look at how the other writer presents the same idea.

Explain how the evidence shows that the writer of the second text has a similar, or contrasting, viewpoint.

Answering Question 6

Getting it right

Use evidence from both texts to compare the writers' views on the theme of the question.

> Both texts present the lives of the rich through the eyes of their hard-working staff. In Text 1, the writer talks about the drivers, servants, orchestra, chefs and bar staff. In Text 2, the writer observes the extravagance of the superyachts and contrasts it with how hard life is for the staff that work on board them.

✓ The first paragraph presents a similarity between the texts. Both similarities and differences are valid.

✗ Although the point is valid, the student could say 'a variety of staff' to be more concise.

> Text 1 uses vivid imagery to show how busy the staff are. The drivers drive cars that 'scampered like a brisk yellow bug'. Text 2 talks about how the 'Crew will wake up to serve breakfast and then stay until the last guest has gone to bed, meaning days can be up to 20 hours'.

✓ The student has used subject-specific terminology when giving their evidence.

✓ This quotation supports the point and is not too long.

✗ The evidence does support the point being made, but it is quite long. An in-line quotation would be more sophisticated and take less time.

> The simile in Text 1 gives the impression of drivers going back and forth to fetch guests. The verb 'scampered' and the adjective 'brisk' create a sense of speed. In Text 2 the days are long; the writer speaks about working from breakfast until the last guest has gone to bed, showing how long and hard the days are for the crew.

✓ This is another example of subject-specific terminology.

✓ Here the focusing in on specific words creates more depth to the answer.

✓ The student has used paraphrasing to give relevant evidence.

✓ This is a good explanation of the effect the writer has created.

TOP TIP

This question is worth 16 marks. To be successful in Question 6, write detailed paragraphs giving accurate explanations and comparing across both texts.

TOP TIP

Always make sure you are comparing the two texts to one another, not just talking about one at a time.

Understanding Section B

Section B of your exam paper will require you to choose between two creative writing questions. You must answer Question 7 **or** Question 8.

How does Question 7 work?

Use language creatively. Your piece can be set anywhere, include any characters and be about anything you like, either real or imagined.

Question 7 will always provide you with a line to begin a piece of imaginative writing. You don't need to copy the first line into your answer booklet but you must make sure that your story continues from that line.

*7 Write an <u>imaginative piece</u> that starts with the line:

'I never wanted a party. I would rather have run away and hidden in my room.'

*Your response will be marked for the accurate and appropriate use of vocabulary, spelling, punctuation and grammar.

(40 marks)

You will be marked for the quality of your spelling, punctuation and grammar so try to write accurately and carefully.

You will be marked on your use of vocabulary.

How do I use the first line to come up with an idea?

You will need to spend some time coming up with a story that you are comfortable writing – the first line is there to inspire you.

The question asks you to produce a piece of 'imaginative writing'. This can mean anything from a story you have made up, to a description of something you have experienced in real life. The important thing is how you write your answer.

TOP TIP

When you are in an exam, you have a limited amount of time. However, this does not mean you have to write the first thing that comes into your head. If you need to, explore a few different ideas before you begin your plan.

How long should I spend?

Questions 7 or 8 are worth 50 per cent of your mark. You should spend about 45 minutes of the total exam time answering **one** of these questions.

What do Questions 7 and 8 assess?

- ☑ Questions 7 and 8 test Assessment Objectives 5 and 6.
- ☑ You need to write clearly and imaginatively.
- ☑ You must organise your ideas and structure your answer.
- ☑ You will be rewarded for using a range of vocabulary and correct spelling, grammar and punctuation.

Understanding Section B

How does Question 8 work?

You can write about something that has actually happened, or you can make something up.

You will have a choice of two photographs to look at. These are provided for inspiration – you can use them for ideas or just to give you a general place to begin.

*8 Write about a time when you, or someone you know, celebrated a special occasion.

Your response could be real or imagined.

You **may** wish to base your response on one of the images or use any ideas of your own.

Your response will be marked for the accurate and appropriate use of vocabulary, spelling, punctuation and grammar.

(40 marks)

Alternatively, you can come up with your own ideas, based on real-life experiences. Or you might be inspired by the texts you have read in Section A – you must not copy from them though.

You will be rewarded for the range of vocabulary you use and for your spelling, grammar and punctuation.

How are Questions 7 and 8 marked?

You will be marked on your ability to produce a convincing piece of imaginative writing.

- ✓ Marks will be allocated for how you organise your answer and how you present your ideas.
- ✓ You can improve your answer by using varied and interesting vocabulary and punctuation.
- ✓ You will be rewarded for accurate spelling, grammar and punctuation.

Answering Section B

There is a lot to consider when preparing to answer an exam question that asks you to write a long imaginative piece.

Reading the question

Read both questions carefully before you decide which one to choose.

EITHER

*7   Write an imaginative piece that starts with the line:

'I never wanted a party. I would rather have run away and hidden in my room.'

Your response will be marked for the accurate and appropriate use of vocabulary, spelling, punctuation and grammar.

OR

*8   Write about a time when you, or someone you know, celebrated a special occasion.

Your response could be real or imagined.

You **may** wish to base your response on one of the images or use any ideas of your own.

Your response will be marked for the accurate and appropriate use of vocabulary, spelling, punctuation and grammar.

(40 marks)

If you choose Question 7, make sure you continue your answer from the first line provided.

Both questions give you the option of making up a story or writing about something that happened to you in real life.

In Question 8, you can choose to use one of the pictures to inspire your writing or come up with your own ideas.

Both Questions 7 and 8 are worth 40 marks. You need to choose only one of them. You will be asked to indicate your choice on the exam paper.

Section B questions will always be linked to the theme of the texts you read for Section A.

Making a choice

Section B of Paper 2 gives you two questions to choose from. It might seem daunting to have choices, especially when you are in an exam with a limited amount of time.

One of the best ways to narrow down your choice is to have plenty of practice before the exam with both question types and find which suits you better. Practise writing from different points of view, and try out different tones – humorous, mysterious, adventurous.

Audience

Think about who is going to read your writing. In Paper 1, you will write for a specific audience, but in Paper 2 you can write for a general audience. This means you don't need to make your writing fit a certain set of rules.

TOP TIP

Read page 41 for more detail on the form and structure of imaginative writing.

Answering Section B

The importance of planning

Once you have chosen a question you need to plan your answer. You will be given space on your exam paper to write a plan. Don't be tempted to jump straight into writing.

Planning your answer before you start writing:

- helps you to organise your ideas
- gives you something to refer to as you write your answer
- enables you to develop your idea into something that has a beginning, a middle and an end
- allows you to think about where your idea is heading.

> Your plan will be invaluable to you in writing an effective response.

Planning your answer – steps to success

1 | Brainstorm your ideas.

Quickly note down all the ideas you can think of that relate to the question you have chosen. Decide on your best idea.

2 | Decide on characters and setting.

Think about where your piece will be set and who the characters are. Decide whether you will write about real people and places, or whether you will make them up. You will need to make these decisions before you begin writing.

3 | Content – beginning

You need to decide whether you are telling the story from a particular character's point of view, and whether you are going to use the first person (e.g. I woke up) or the third person (e.g. he woke up).

4 | Content – middle

Develop the action of your story and describe what happens to the character(s).

If you are writing a description, come up with 3–4 specific elements of the subject that you will focus on. For example, if you are writing about an event, you might choose (a) where it took place; (b) who else was there; (c) what the food and drinks were like; (d) the atmosphere.

5 | Content – end

You will need to decide how to end your piece. If it's a story, it needs to have an ending that makes sense. If it's a description or monologue, come to a conclusion. All endings should be satisfactory to the reader.

For more detail on writing an imaginative piece, go to pages 37 and 39–43.

Answering Section B

Now you need to write your answer. Make sure you think about your language choices as you write, and pay attention to your structure.

Writing your answer

Section B is worth 50 per cent of your mark for Paper 2 so you need to spend about 45 minutes on Question 7 or 8. Make sure you are progressing from one point of your plan to the next.

- ✓ In the first paragraph, try to set the scene. Give a sense of the place and time and, if it's a narrative piece, who the main character is and what they want.
- ✓ Once you have set the scene, get straight into the story. Perhaps something happens that makes your character act. In a descriptive piece, set the scene then move on to your next idea.
- ✓ Do not spend too long on any one part of your story, particularly on events or conversations that do not move the story along.

How should I spend my time?

While it's tempting to leap straight in and begin writing, organising your time should help you to remain calm and focused.

You are advised to spend 45 minutes on Section B. Here are some different ways you might use this time.

Student A

2 minutes choosing a question

5 minutes brainstorming

5 minutes writing a brief plan

30 minutes writing

3 minutes checking

Student B

5 minutes brainstorming two different ideas

10 minutes writing a plan for the best idea

25 minutes writing

5 minutes checking

What to include

Think about these elements:

- **Vocabulary**: try to avoid using simple words – choose interesting and vivid vocabulary instead.
- **Language devices**: to interest and engage your reader, use imagery (similes, metaphors, personification), sound effects (alliteration, onomatopoeia) and language based around the senses.
- **Structure**: think about using an unusual structure to surprise or intrigue your reader. For example, start in the middle and then flashback to the beginning to see how the character ended up where they are now. Or use different formats like diary entries. Or use one word or a short sentence for your opening or ending.
- **Spelling**: be careful with your spelling throughout, paying close attention to homonyms in particular (words that sound the same but are spelt differently, for example 'their', 'there' and 'they're').
- **Punctuation**: use a range of punctuation to engage your reader and to slow down, or speed up, the pace of your story.

Can I change my story as I go along?

- ✓ Your plan is there to guide you, not to restrict you. Use it, update it, or even disregard it once you are confident you know where your story is going.
- ✓ Check your plan every so often to make sure you stay on track.
- ✓ If you think of something extra, see where it fits, and amend your plan. Check that your ending will still make sense, or tweak it to fit the new idea.
- ✓ Finish your piece of writing with an appropriate ending to show that you have thought through your idea.

Answering Section B

Getting it right

Even though you have the freedom to create something new in Section B, you must still be sure to connect it to the question. Your writing can be imaginary, but you need to show that you are responding to one of the questions rather than coming up with something completely disconnected. Look at the selection of opening lines for the question below.

7   Write an imaginative piece that starts with the line:

'I never wanted a party. I would rather have run away and hidden in my room.'

My mum insisted though and I could hardly ignore a party where the guest of honour was a mermaid. I couldn't wait for the party to start.

✓ This sentence follows on neatly from the first line.

✓ This is an interesting twist, and sets up an expectation for a surprising story.

✗ This bit does not work. The character goes from not wanting a party to being very excited, without any explanation about their change of heart.

The problem was, I was turning 16, and everyone has a party when they're 16, don't they?

✓ This works well as it develops the idea from the first line, and shows a potential source of conflict.

✓ This gives an impression of who the main character in the story is, and their feelings about the situation.

Ryan woke up one morning and found his sister had gone missing.

✗ This sentence does not flow well from the first line of the question. It doesn't appear to be connected.

✗ It sounds like it could be an exciting, mysterious story – however, it does not fit with the question.

But when there's a dragon hiding in your room already, sometimes you have to choose the safest option.

✓ A brilliant response to the opening line. This next line connects directly to the question, but also surprises the reader. It presents a very different world and suggests the type of story that the reader can expect.

Checking your answer

Try to leave enough time to go back over your answer and check for spelling mistakes. This also gives you the chance to improve your story if you have time.

✓ Check spelling, grammar and punctuation. These are all rewarded, so try to be as careful as you can. If you spot a spelling mistake, cross it through and write the correct spelling above.

✓ If you need to add more to a sentence or paragraph, use an asterisk (*) to indicate where you want to add words, then use another asterisk at the bottom of the page or in the margin before the extra words. Number the asterisks if necessary.

✓ Improve your vocabulary – if you spot a boring word like 'good' or 'nice', try to think of an alternative to add interest to your writing.

✗ Don't put aside too much time for checking – it's much quicker to read than to write, so make sure you prioritise completing your work.

Time

Unlocking the question

Find the key words that tell you what explicit information you are looking out for.

Hint

Answer with short quotations or paraphrase from the text.

Watch out!

The possible answers will be contained within the line numbers given.

 Time

You should spend about **8–10 minutes** answering Question 2.

Unlocking the question

Read the question carefully to find out what to look for in the text extract given.

Hint

As you read, underline any language features you notice.

Unlocking the question

You are asked to use examples and relevant subject terminology. Make sure you find evidence for your points and see if you can name any language devices that you have identified.

English Language 2.0
Paper 2: Contemporary Texts

SECTION A

Reading

You should spend about 1 hour 10 minutes on this section.

Read Text 1 in the Source Booklet provided and answer Questions 1–2.

Write your answers in the spaces provided.

1 From lines 3–5, identify **one** sign that the ship is flooding.

(1 mark)

....

....

2 Read this extract.

> The ship shook and there was that sound, the monstrous metallic burp. What was it? Was it the collective scream of humans and animals protesting their oncoming death? Was it the ship itself giving up the ghost? I fell over. I got to my feet. I looked overboard again. The sea was rising. The waves were getting closer. We were sinking fast.
>
> I clearly heard monkeys shrieking. Something was shaking the deck, a gaur – an Indian wild ox – exploded out of the rain and thundered by me, terrified, out of control, berserk. I looked at it, dumbstruck and amazed. Who in God's name had let it out?

In this extract, how does the writer use language to present Pi's experience of the ship sinking?

Use examples from the extract and relevant subject terminology.

(6 marks)

....

....

....

....

(blank lined answer space)

Watch out!

Be careful not to write too much or you will run out of time for the other questions.

TOP TIP

If you recognise a language device or part of speech, try to work out if it is relevant to answering the question.

Unlocking the question

You will always be asked 'how' the writer has used language. This means making the link between the words and phrases they have chosen, and the effect they have on the reader.

LEARN IT!

Revise language devices to give yourself the best chance of spotting them in your exam.

Hint

Turn to pages 115–118 to remind yourself about Question 2.

Watch out!

Keep your quotations short and focused to save time.

Hint

Zoom in on specific words and phrases to analyse their effect on the reader.

Time

Spend **1–2 minutes** on
Question 3.

**Unlocking
the question**

You are searching for
one piece of implicit
information in the text
given here.

Hint

Look out for vocabulary
in the extract that fits
with the theme of
the question.

Watch out!

There will be more than
one possible answer, but
make sure you identify
only one thing.

 **Time**

You should spend about
15 minutes on Question 4.

**Unlocking
the question**

Question 4 asks you to
look at the **whole** text. You
will need to consider both
language and structure.

Hint

Think about how the text
is structured: how it
begins and ends; what
changes. Consider why
the writer presented it in
this order.

**Unlocking
the question**

You must give evidence
from the text to support
your answers.

Read Text 2 in the Source Booklet provided and answer Questions 3–4.

Write your answers in the spaces provided.

3   Read this extract.

> I retired at 10.30 p.m. to be awakened about 11.40 by a violent jar.
> I had the impression that the steamer had been struck on her side
> with sufficient force to move her bodily in a lateral direction. I hastily
> threw on a long overcoat and left my cabin to find a large number of
> passengers, all anxiously enquiring what had happened.

From the extract, identify **one** thing that suggests there is something to
worry about on the ship.

(1 mark)

....

....

4   The writer describes the sinking of the *Titanic*.

How does the writer try to interest and engage the reader?

You should include:

- the writer's use of language
- the writer's use of structure
- the effect on the reader.

Use examples from the whole text and relevant subject terminology.

(10 marks)

....

....

....

....

....

....

[ruled answer lines]

Think about how the text makes you feel as a reader. See if you can find examples in the text of words, phrases and sentence structures that have contributed to this emotion.

Watch out!

Make sure you develop your points – your answer should not be a list of ten things about the text.

TOP TIP

Develop your points with in-depth explanations of the effects of language and structure on the reader.

LEARN IT!

Use P–E–E (Point–Evidence–Explain) paragraphs to write a successful answer to this question.

Watch out!

Be careful to focus on a few specific points, rather than trying to talk about everything you've noticed in the text.

Hint

Aim to use short quotations that support your point – don't rewrite long sections of the text.

LEARN IT!

Use subject-specific terminology.

Questions 5–6 are on both Text 1 and Text 2.

Remember to refer to both texts in your answers.

Write your answer in the space provided.

5   Text 1 and Text 2 both show experiences of ships sinking. The experiences are different, but they share similarities.

Write a summary giving **three** separate ways the experiences are similar.

Support **each separate similarity** with evidence from **both** texts.

(6 marks)

....

....

....

....

....

....

....

....

....

....

....

....

....

....

....

....

....

....

....

....

....

⏱ **Time**

You should spend **8–10 minutes** answering Question 5.

Unlocking the question

Find three separate similarities between the two texts. These could be similarities in themes, actions, people and places.

TOP TIP

The theme of the two texts will always be linked. Work out what the links are and use these as a basis for answering Question 5.

Unlocking the question

For **each** of your similarities, give evidence from **both** texts.

Watch out!

Make sure you **don't** talk about **differences** between the texts in Question 5.

TOP TIP

Make a point and back it up with evidence from Text 1 and Text 2.

TOP TIP

Use language such as 'both', 'similarly', and 'just as... so...' to compare the two texts.

TOP TIP

The texts are from different time periods, and one is fiction while the other is non-fiction. Consider how these differences might contribute to the writers' different perspectives.

Unlocking the question

You need to think about the main ideas the writers have used within the texts.

Hint

You can talk about both similarities and differences in Question 6. You've already thought about similarities for Question 5, so a good starting point could be to think about what is different about the two texts.

Unlocking the question

In Question 6 you need to consider the writers' points of view on the theme. This means how they react to it, and their perspective on it.

Hint

See if the writers have written in the first or third person and consider if this has an effect on the reader.

6   Compare the writers' ideas and perspectives on going through a frightening experience at sea.

You should compare the writers':

• main ideas

• points of view

• presentation of these ideas and views.

Use examples from both texts to support your comparison.

(16 marks)

....

....

....

....

....

....

....

....

....

....

....

....

....

....

....

....

....

....

....

....
....
....
....
....
....
....
....
....
....
....
....
....
....
....
....
....
....
....
....
....
....
....
....
....
....

Watch out!

You must refer to both texts for Question 6.

Hint

Turn to pages 129–132 to remind yourself about Question 6.

Unlocking the question

You need to consider the presentation of both writers' ideas and perspectives – this means the methods they have used to achieve an effect on the reader. Consider tone, imagery and type of sentence, and the effect these create.

TOP TIP

Picture the scene in your mind as you read – think about which words and phrases help you imagine what is happening.

LEARN IT!

Revise key vocabulary and sentence starters for comparing two texts. See page 129.

Watch out!

Try to avoid talking about one text at a time. Refer to one text, then compare or contrast it with the other.

Hint

Think about the overall tone of the texts – whether they are positive or negative – and what the main emotion is. Consider how this is conveyed.

Hint

Develop in-depth paragraphs, comparing ideas and perspectives across both texts, and discussing broader themes as well as zooming in on specific details.

⏱ Time

You should spend about **45 minutes** on Section B.

Unlocking the question

Read Questions 7 and 8 carefully and think about which one you are more comfortable with.

TOP TIP

You can write about something real or imagined. If one of the questions reminds you of something that's happened to you or someone you know in real life, that might be a good choice.

Unlocking the question

Questions 7 and 8 are worth 40 marks, so it is important to spend time thinking and planning your answer before you begin writing.

Hint

Remind yourself about Questions 7 and 8 on pages 133–134.

Watch out!

In Section B, your spelling, punctuation and grammar will be marked. Make sure you take care with your writing, thinking carefully about tricky spellings and using a variety of punctuation.

SECTION B

Writing

Answer ONE question. You should spend about 45 minutes on this section.

Write your answer in the space provided.

EITHER

*7 Write an imaginative piece that starts with the line:

'I had fought every day of my life to get here. I couldn't give up now.'

*Your response will be marked for the accurate and appropriate use of vocabulary, spelling, punctuation and grammar.

(40 marks)

OR

*8 Write about a time when you, or someone you know, dealt with a difficult situation.

Your response could be real or imagined.

You **may** wish to base your response on one of the images or use any ideas of your own.

*Your response will be marked for the accurate and appropriate use of vocabulary, spelling, punctuation and grammar.

(40 marks)

BEGIN YOUR ANSWER ON PAGE 151

Unlocking the question

The photographs are provided to inspire you. You could choose to write about the character in the photograph; or to imagine a story based in the same setting as one of the photographs; or to write about something completely different.

TOP TIP

You have several choices available to you for Section B. Spend a minute or two jotting down your initial reactions to the questions to see which one feels like the best option for you.

Unlocking the question

Question 7 provides you with a first line. Spend a moment or two jotting down possible stories that could begin with that line.

LEARN IT!

Revise the different forms of writing that you can produce for Section B – narrative, descriptive and monologue. See page 135.

**Unlocking
the question**

You will be given a space
to indicate which question
you have chosen, and a
space to plan your work.

Time

Spend about **10 minutes**
planning your work.

TOP TIP

Think about your beginning,
middle and end before
you start writing.
Focus on a main event,
action or description.

TOP TIP

Use your planning space
to work out who your main
character is going to be
and where your story is
going to be set. You need
to think about this even
if you are writing from
experience. Describing a
setting in detail, even if
you know it well, will help
create a picture in your
reader's mind.

TOP TIP

Practise using a variety of
vocabulary when you revise.
Use a thesaurus to find
and learn synonyms for
common words.

Hint

Think about your opening
and closing: how you
will grab the reader's
attention at the start and
then make sure they are
satisfied with the ending.

Indicate which question you are answering by marking a cross in the
box ☒. If you change your mind, put a line through the box ☒ and then
indicate your new question with a cross ☒.

Chosen question number: **Question 7**   ☒   **Question 8**   ☒

Plan your answer to Section B here:

Write your answer to Section B here:

....

....

....

....

....

....

....

....

....

....

[ruled answer lines — blank]

Think about how you want your reader to feel when they read your piece of writing. Use vocabulary and language devices such as imagery that will help them to feel the way you, or your character, feels.

Watch out!

Don't skip the planning section – you will find it makes writing your answer much easier.

Unlocking the question

Think about your audience. You can write for adults or young people your own age.

TOP TIP

Use a selection of punctuation to improve your writing.

Hint

Think about pacing your writing – if you want your reader to feel as though lots is happening, use short sentences, snappy dialogue and short paragraphs. If you are writing a more descriptive passage, or a slower-paced piece, use longer sentences.

Unlocking the question

You have 45 minutes for Section B – you could spend **10 minutes** planning, **30 minutes** writing and **5 minutes** checking.

TOP TIP

Use some of the five senses to enrich your writing. Engage your reader by thinking about the sounds, smells and tastes in your story, and describe how things feel.

Watch out!

If you're writing a descriptive piece, try to shift the focus of the description from one paragraph to the next to keep your reader interested.

Hint

Consider using single-sentence or even single-word paragraphs for emphasis at important moments in your story.

Hint

Interest and engage your reader by using different techniques, for example dialogue, internal thoughts including rhetorical questions, and even different sections so you can move through time, making your story structure more interesting.

TOP TIP

Try to leave 5 minutes spare to check through your work. Look out for basic vocabulary and try to exchange simple words for more interesting ones. Add extra sentences if they will improve your story.

Continue writing on your own separate pieces of paper.

SECTION A

Reading

You should spend about 1 hour 10 minutes on this section.

Read Text 1 in the Source Booklet provided and answer Questions 1–2.

Write your answers in the spaces provided.

1   From lines 3–5, identify **one** sign that the ship is flooding.

(1 mark)

Water was 'surging from below'.

The student uses direct quotation from the source text.

The answer is concise and directly answers the question.

Alternative answers

Answers to Question 1 could also include:

• The narrator could see 'lots of water'.

• Water was blocking his way.

• The stairs 'vanished into watery darkness'.

• There is water on the stairs.

• The narrator 'couldn't believe his eyes' as the water should not be there.

Hint

Read the notes below, then look at the sample answer on page 156.

2   Read this extract.

> The ship shook and there was that sound, the monstrous metallic burp. What was it? Was it the collective scream of humans and animals protesting their oncoming death? Was it the ship itself giving up the ghost? I fell over. I got to my feet. I looked overboard again. The sea was rising. The waves were getting closer. We were sinking fast.
>
> I clearly heard monkeys shrieking. Something was shaking the deck, a gaur – an Indian wild ox – exploded out of the rain and thundered by me, terrified, out of control, berserk. I looked at it, dumbstruck and amazed. Who in God's name had let it out?

In this extract, how does the writer use language to present Pi's experience of the ship sinking?

Use examples from the extract and relevant subject terminology.

(6 marks)

Writing a good answer

Good answers will:
- pick out a language feature or device and accurately explain how it links to the topic in the question
- use evidence from the text to support points
- use relevant subject terminology to demonstrate knowledge
- explain **how** the writer has used language to present the question topic.

Relevant points may include:
- use of sensory language (for example: 'the monstrous metallic burp'; monkeys 'shrieking'; 'shaking the deck') to help the reader imagine how it felt to be there
- personification of the ship to help readers imagine the scene
- use of alliteration, such as 'monstrous metallic burp', to draw attention to the sound and emphasise it
- the verb 'exploded' and the adjectives 'terrified' and 'berserk', which describe the behaviour of the ox and help the reader to imagine how frightened the narrator must have been.

Q2: sample answer

The writer uses sensory language to help convey a 'sense of the terror the narrator experiences as the ship is sinking. The description of a mysterious sound as a 'monstrous metallic burp' helps the reader to imagine the sound. The alliteration of 'monstrous metallic' and the personification of the sound as a 'burp' help to create an image in the reader's mind. The adjective 'monstrous' emphasises the terrifying nature of the sound.

Furthermore, the narrator's use of the strong verb 'exploded' to describe the wild ox appearing gives a sense of how sudden and shocking it was for him.

The narrator asks questions such as 'what was it?' to give a sense of his confusion. He does not understand what is happening, and the language he uses indicates this to the reader, who shares in his confusion as he tries to find possible explanations for the sounds he is hearing.

The student introduces the first point and identifies the type of language device being used.

Here is a link back to the question by describing the feelings of the narrator.

A concise, well-chosen quotation is incorporated into the sentence.

The student gives an explanation of the effect of the language device.

The answer has more in-depth analysis of specific language features and the effects they create.

The answer continues with more examples of language and how they convey Pi's experience.

A very strong answer because...

This answer focuses initially on one quotation but goes into depth to describe the effects of various language devices. It remains tightly focused on the question by referring back to the feelings experienced by the narrator. The student uses short, well-chosen quotations as evidence. They then focus on specific words and phrases to examine their effects on the reader. The answer makes confident use of language-specific terminology, for example 'sensory language', 'alliteration' and 'adjective', and the terms are used accurately and in context.

Read Text 2 in the Source Booklet provided and answer Questions 3–4.

Write your answers in the spaces provided.

3 Read this extract.

> I retired at 10.30 p.m. to be awakened about 11.40 by a violent jar. I had the impression that the steamer had been struck on her side with sufficient force to move her bodily in a lateral direction – I hastily threw on a long overcoat and left my cabin to find a large number of passengers, all anxiously enquiring what had happened.

From the extract, identify **one** thing that suggests there is something to worry about on the ship.

(1 mark)

The student accurately paraphrases language from the text to answer the question.

The answer is brief and uses the correct information from the extract.

> The writer woke up because he felt something hit the ship.

Alternative answers

Answers to Question 3 could also include:

- The writer was 'awakened' by a 'violent jar'.
- The writer thought that the ship had been hit by something.
- The writer thinks the 'steamer had been struck on her side'.
- The passengers are anxious.
- The writer and other passengers don't know what has happened.

4   The writer describes the sinking of the *Titanic*.

How does the writer try to interest and engage the reader?

You should include:

- the writer's use of language

- the writer's use of structure

- the effect on the reader.

Use examples from the whole text and relevant subject terminology.

(10 marks)

Hint

Read the notes below, then look at the sample answer on page 159.

Writing a good answer

Good answers will:

- include points about **both** language and structure
- make links between the points and how they interest and engage the reader
- use evidence from the text to support points
- use relevant subject terminology to add detail
- refer to examples from the whole text
- develop points into paragraphs.

Relevant points may include:

- chronological report of events, use of time indicators and numbers, to convey information to the reader
- increase in tension from the initial confusion through to the danger to the lives of the passengers
- use of adverbs: 'anxiously' to describe the feelings of the passengers; 'rapidly' to describe the speed the narrator walked, to give a sense of the danger
- long sentences giving clear and detailed description of how the passengers were loaded in lifeboats to help the reader imagine what it must have been like to be there
- use of strong adjectives and nouns to give a sense of the danger as they are leaving the boat: 'perilous' and 'destruction'
- use of contrast to give a sense of the calm water and having made it to safety at the end.

The first point is clearly introduced and relates to structure.

A link is made to how the specific structure of the text will interest the reader.

Here is good use of paraphrasing to avoid multiple quotations.

The second paragraph introduces a point about language and its effect.

Brief quotations are given as part of a sentence.

The student uses subject-specific terminology.

The student clearly explains the effects of the writer's language on the reader, and links back to the question.

Paragraphs show the organisation of ideas and allow development of points.

The final example includes evidence, subject-specific terminology and explanation of effect on the reader.

Q4: sample answer

The writer structures the piece chronologically. This is interesting for a reader because they can better understand what happened when the Titanic sank from the perspective of someone who was there. The writer uses specific data, for example times, the numbers of the boats, and heights and distances to allow the reader to accurately imagine what it must have been like to be there.

The writer uses language to engage the reader, and to convey a sense of tension. At the beginning, when the passengers do not know what is happening, they are waiting 'anxiously' and the writer is walking 'rapidly'. These two adverbs engage the reader as they offer a perspective on the danger that the passengers sensed approaching. Later on in the text the writer's choice of language shows how much more serious the danger has become. The use of the adjective 'perilous' and the noun 'destruction' show that the situation is very serious and the reader is engaged by this increase in tension.

Finally the contrast at the end of the text with the use of the simile 'as calm as the waters of a smooth flowing river' to describe the ocean, shows how lucky the survivors are to be away from the danger. This would give the reader a sense of satisfaction and relief.

A very strong answer because...

This answer uses in-depth paragraphs to make valid points about the text. It makes use of evidence, selecting between quotations where they can be kept short and concise, and paraphrasing where this is more appropriate. The student combines discussion of structure with comments on language features, and describes their effects on the reader throughout. The answer focuses on the question wording, specifically on how the writer 'interests and engages' the reader, and stays focused throughout. The use of sophisticated vocabulary and subject-specific terminology gives the student the opportunity to improve the quality of their response.

Questions 5–6 are on both Text 1 and Text 2.

Remember to refer to both texts in your answers.

Write your answer in the space provided.

Hint

Read the notes below, then look at the sample answer on page 161.

5   Text 1 and Text 2 both show experiences of ships sinking. The experiences are different, but they share similarities.

Write a summary giving **three** separate ways the experiences are similar.

Support **each separate similarity** with evidence from **both** texts.

(6 marks)

**Writing a
good answer**

Good answers will:

- find three different similarities between the two texts
- use evidence from both texts to support points
- keep answers concise and focused.

Relevant points may include:

- in both texts, the narrators show fear, for example 'frightened and incredulous' (Text 1); 'anxiously' and 'destruction' (Text 2)
- the water is described as threatening, for example 'raging, frothing and boiling' (Text 1); 'immense volume of water' (Text 2)
- the narrators in both texts describe a lack of help. In Text 1: 'where were the officers and the crew?'; in Text 2: 'we had no officer in our boat to direct us'
- both texts describe the physical movement of the ships as they sink. Text 1: 'There was a noticeable incline going from bow to stern'; Text 2: 'the steamer had settled several feet into the water at her bow'.

The first point is made, stating the similarity, using the sentence starter 'both texts show.'

Brief in-line quotations give supporting evidence.

The student uses the comparative sentence starter 'similarly'.

The student gives a second similarity with short quotations for evidence.

The final similarity is given, and is different from the other two.

Evidence is given from both texts to answer the question.

Q5: sample answer

'Both texts show the fear of the narrators. In Text 1 the narrator explains how scared he is, using words such as 'frightened and incredulous'. Similarly, Text 2 uses words such as 'anxiously' and 'destruction' to describe the increasing level of fear.

Both texts show the water as threatening, for example 'raging, frothing and boiling' in Text 1 and 'immense volume of water' in Text 2.

In both texts, the narrators describe being unable to find officers to provide guidance and safety. In Text 1 the narrator enquires 'Where were the officers and the crew?' and in Text 2 the writer states 'We had no officer in our boat to direct us'.

A very strong answer because...

This answer addresses the question directly and does not add unnecessary detail. The answer gives three separate similarities, and supports each with evidence from both texts. The student stays focused on the question and does not explain the writers' methods or give differences instead of similarities. The quotations used are brief and concise and support the similarities given.

6 Compare the writers' ideas and perspectives on going through a frightening experience at sea.

You should compare the writers':

- main ideas

- points of view

- presentation of these ideas and views.

Use examples from both texts to support your comparison.

(16 marks)

Hint

Read the notes below, then look at the sample answer on page 163.

Writing a good answer

Good answers will:

- compare the ideas and points of view presented in both texts
- use evidence from both texts to support comparisons
- discuss the presentation of writers' ideas and points of view
- use comparative language to contrast the two texts
- develop analysis using in-depth paragraphs
- comment on a variety of features including language, structure, tone and form.

Relevant points may include:

- how the texts are structured for impact
- the forms of the texts and how they suit the purpose
- the tones of the two pieces of writing and how these have been created
- discussion of the language used to create effects.

The first point discusses the overall tone of the two texts.

Use of 'whereas' and 'on the other hand' indicates the contrast between the two texts.

The student provides evidence and uses subject-specific terminology.

They explain the effect of the evidence on the reader.

Short quotations are given in-line as part of the sentence.

The answer uses subject-specific terminology accurately and explains its effects.

The point is explored in more depth.

A second paragraph begins a new point.

The point is expanded upon using contrasting examples from both texts.

The second point deals with a similarity in content but discusses how the two writers deal with it differently, using different language devices.

The point is developed with further evidence.

Parts of speech have been picked out and their effects explained.

Q6: sample answer

Both texts tell the story of a shipwreck. However, the narrator in Text 1 conveys a sense of fear and confusion, whereas in Text 2 the mood is much calmer despite the danger. Text 1 uses rhetorical questions such as 'What was this water doing here? Where had it come from?' These help the reader to understand how confused and disorientated the narrator was by the situation. On the other hand, Text 2 states that the passengers waited 'anxiously', and says that the narrator walked 'rapidly' to see his family. Although the adverbs show there is a sense of danger, the narrator is not panicking. This contrasts with the narrator in Text 1 who 'ran to the bridge'; 'fell' and 'got up' – his physical movements also suggest how scared and confused he is.

Both texts describe dangerous things happening in addition to the ships sinking. In Text 1, the narrator describes the 'dangerous wild animals' on board the boat, whereas in Text 2 there is an 'immense volume of water' being thrown from the ship's condenser pump, which threatened those leaving the ship with 'destruction'. In both cases, the language used to describe these dangers shows how much of a threat to life they are. In Text 1 the description of the gaur which 'exploded out of the rain and thundered by me' not only reflects the fear and confusion felt by the narrator, but the use of the strong verbs 'exploded' and 'thundered' also show the reader how much danger the narrator is in. In Text 2 the 'immense force' of the water being thrown from the ship would have 'instantly swamped' the lifeboat. The adverb 'instantly' shows how real the danger was for the survivors.

The accurate descriptions of time, the size of the iceberg, and the lifeboat numbers add to the overall tone in Text 2. This level of detail shows that the narrator had the presence of mind to note all of this information despite his fear, and it gives the reader a clear sense of what was happening. In Text 1 the reader feels as disorientated as the narrator due to the writer's use of short sentences such as 'I fell. I got up.' and 'I shouted. They turned.' These add to the pace of the writing which makes the reader feel the same panic and confusion as the narrator.

For the final point, paraphrasing introduces the evidence.

The student explains why the point is relevant.

They further explain how this point impacts on the reader.

Reference to the other text and how it contrasts on this point.

This point refers to the structure of the text.

Again, the overall effect of the structural feature is explained, along with its impact on the reader.

A very strong answer because...

This answer begins with a clear point, and goes on to develop it through the use of various examples. In each paragraph, the student deals with a specific example, which they then explore in great depth, picking out different quotations from throughout both texts to support their opinions. The answer makes accurate and extensive use of subject-specific terminology. The student spends time not only explaining the effect of the language or structural device they have highlighted, but also exploring its impact on the reader. Overall, the answer focuses on the differing tone of the two texts, and through the exploration of various ideas and devices, it develops sophisticated points to explain how these tones are created.

Hint

Turn to pages 133–138 to remind yourself about answering Questions 7 and 8.

Hint

Read the notes below, then look at the sample answer on page 166.

SECTION B

Writing

EITHER

*7 Write an imaginative piece that starts with the line:

'I had fought every day of my life to get here. I couldn't give up now.'

*Your response will be marked for the accurate and appropriate use of vocabulary, spelling, punctuation and grammar.

OR

*8 Write about a time when you, or someone you know, dealt with a difficult situation.

Your response could be real or imagined.

You **may** wish to base your response on one of the images or use any ideas of your own.

*Your response will be marked for the accurate and appropriate use of vocabulary, spelling, punctuation and grammar.

(40 marks)

Writing a good answer

Good answers will:

• use the planning space provided to develop a plan with a beginning, middle and end
• think about the question to come up with an imaginative answer
• use varied vocabulary
• pay close attention to spelling, grammar and punctuation throughout
• use interesting language and a variety of structural features to interest and engage the reader
• maintain an appropriate tone and style.

Chosen question number: **Question 7** ☒   **Question 8** ☐

Plan your answer to Section B here:

Rider in a bike race – struggling up a hill. First person..

Who: Rider. Trying to finish the race.

Describe the scenery. British – hills, weather – describe – wind pushing him back.

Describe the climb – physical pain – legs burning/screaming etc. – also psychological – just wants to stop.

Sensory language – shouts of the crowd – sound of the helicopter, motorbikes. Smells: countryside – petrol fumes from lead motorbikes. Sweat. Muscle cream. Taste: metallic – from over-exerting himself. Touch: feel of the handlebars solid in his grip, the bike carrying him up the hill.

Beginning – how the day started. Contrast – hopeful, feeling good. Looking back.

Middle – present moment – the main struggle up the hill.

End – he makes it – describe crowd cheering, his feelings of accomplishment and joy.

Use the space provided to develop a plan. Consider the general idea for the piece and what perspective to write it from.

Consider who the main character in the piece will be and what their goals are.

Consider the setting for the story and what it is like there.

Use of all five senses. Jot down ideas here to refer back to when writing.

Personification of bike.

Plan for what will happen at the beginning, in the middle and at the end of the story, to keep the writing on track.

Write your answer to Section B here:

Q7: sample answer

The opening line follows on from the line given in the question, and creates a sense of the mood.

The answer makes good use of long and short paragraphs for impact.

Language devices are used for effect, such as this rhetorical question.

There are different types of punctuation to interest the reader.

New paragraph for a change in tone.

Personification of the wind helps the reader imagine the scene.

Imagery such as this simile engages the reader.

Strong verbs, simile and personification are all used in this strong piece of imagery.

Repetition helps to emphasise the rider's exhaustion.

Strong verbs help the reader imagine the pain the rider is in.

Strong statement to reflect the character's negative feelings.

Sensory language is used here along with onomatopoeia to make the reader appreciate what it felt and sounded like to be there.

Repetition and short sentences show the rider's determination and so interest and engage the reader.

It had started so well. The sun streaming down over the Cumbrian hills and warming my face as I waited for the race to begin. The other riders on my team were all in good spirits, the sounds of laughter echoing in the valley and the smell of muscle cream and freshly laundered kit pungent on the air as we took our spots on the start line.

If I had known what lay ahead, would I have gone through with it?

We moved as one through the undulating countryside, one hundred riders all with the same goal: to win. Me? I simply wanted to make it to the end of the day in one piece. I had heard tales about this hill, the biggest one we would face in the race, and my hands shook on the handlebars as I imagined it rearing up ahead of me. I shook it off. There were many miles to ride before we reached it.

Then the weather turned. The wind picked up, whipping the flags the crowd waved aloft and yanking at the fabric, and the rain came down in sheets. I shivered and gripped harder, my bike working beneath me, solid and steady despite my growing dread.

Then there it was. The hill, rising up like a wall in front of me. The landscape was barren and unforgiving. There was no way around it. Only over it.

The clouds hung low like a dark frown and the wind howled in my ears. I couldn't see, couldn't think. My legs screamed as I fought my way up the climb. I feared it would never end. Where were my teammates? Had they left me behind? I didn't think I would make it. Not up the hill, not home. I would be stuck here, in purgatory, forever.

As the yells of the crowd resounded and the rhythmic clatter of the helicopter competed with the wind, I saw the most welcome sight: the peak. Marked with flags and surrounded by a cluster of spectators, I was so close now I could almost taste it. I could do this. I would do this.

I crested the hill and began the long descent as the sun burst through the clouds. I was flying, the wind with me now, urging me on, the choke of the motorbikes and cheers of the fans pushing me faster. I rode harder and faster, and my muscles sang with the hope that maybe, just maybe, I might be in with a chance.

The finish line was in sight. Was it a mirage? I dropped my head and surged forward like a wave. I crossed the line, and cheers erupted around me. My family rushed to greet me. Their pride was worth more than any prize.

In the end, it didn't matter where I came. I had done it. The longest day of my life was finally over.

The change in weather and personification signal the change in mood.

A metaphor (flying) is used to convey a sense of what the narrator is feeling.

The mood and tone change as the story reaches its climax.

A message or the 'moral' of the story is communicated clearly.

The last line echoes the first line, bringing the story to a satisfying close.

Cut along the dotted lines and staple the texts together to make your own handy anthology. Make sure you keep it safe with your Revision Guide and Workbook.

TEXT 1

This is an extract from a letter sent by Charlotte Brontë to her father. She is telling him about her visit to The Great Exhibition held in London at the Crystal Palace.

Yesterday I went for the second time to the Crystal Palace. It is a wonderful place – vast, strange, new, and impossible to describe. Its grandeur does not consist in **one** thing, but in the unique assemblage of **all** things. Whatever human industry has created, you find there, from the great compartments filled with railway engines and boilers, with mill machinery in full work, with splendid carriages of all kinds, with harness of every description – to the glass-covered and velvet-spread stands loaded with the most gorgeous work of the goldsmith and silversmith, and the carefully guarded caskets full of real diamonds and pearls worth hundreds of thousands of pounds. 5

It seems as if magic only could have gathered this mass of wealth from all the ends of the earth – as if none but supernatural hands could have arranged it thus, with such a blaze and contrast of colours and marvellous power of effect. The multitude filling the great aisles seems ruled and subdued by some invisible influence. Amongst the thirty thousand souls 10 15
that peopled it the day I was there, not one loud noise was to be heard, not one irregular movement seen – the living tide rolls on quietly, with a deep hum like the sea heard from the distance.

Cut along the dotted lines and staple the texts together to make your own handy anthology. Make sure you keep it safe with your Revision Guide and Workbook.

TEXT 2

This is an extract from a letter by Charles Dickens about the execution of two people in London. The letter was published in The Times *newspaper in 1849.*

I was a witness of the execution at Horsemonger-lane. I went there with the intention of observing the crowd gathered to behold it, and I had excellent opportunities of doing so, at intervals all through the night, and continuously from daybreak until after the spectacle was over.

5 I believe that a sight so inconceivably awful as the wickedness and levity[1] of the immense crowd collected at that execution could be imagined by no man, and could be presented in no heathen[2] land under the sun. The horrors of the gibbet[3] and of the crime which brought the wretched murderers to it, faded in my mind before the atrocious bearing, looks and language, of the assembled spectators.

10 When I came upon the scene at midnight, the shrillness of the cries and howls that were raised from time to time made my blood run cold. When the day dawned, thieves, low prostitutes, ruffians and vagabonds of every kind flocked on to the ground, with every variety of offensive and foul behaviour. Fightings, faintings, whistlings, brutal jokes, [disorderly] demonstrations of indecent delight when swooning women were dragged out of the crowd
15 by the police with their dresses disordered, gave a new zest to the general entertainment. When the sun rose brightly it [shone upon] thousands upon thousands of upturned faces, so inexpressibly odious in their brutal mirth or callousness, that a man had cause to feel ashamed of the shape he wore, and to shrink from himself, as fashioned in the image of the Devil.

20 When the two miserable [criminals] who attracted all this ghastly sight about them were turned into the air, there was no more emotion, no more restraint in any of the previous obscenities, than if the name of Christ had never been heard in this world, and there were no belief among men but that they perished like the beasts.

I am solemnly convinced that nothing that ingenuity[4] could devise to be done in this city
25 could work such ruin as one public execution, and I stand astounded and appalled by the wickedness it exhibits. I do not believe that any community can prosper where such a scene of horror and demoralization as was enacted outside Horsemonger-lane Jail is presented at the very doors of good citizens, and is passed by, unknown or forgotten. And when, in our prayers and thanksgivings for the season, we are humbly expressing before God our desire to remove
30 the moral evils of the land, I would ask your readers to consider whether it is not a time to think of this one, and to root it out.

---

[1] *levity* – the treatment of a serious matter with humour and lack of respect

[2] *heathen* – without religion

[3] *gibbet* – a gallows; a structure used to hang people

[4] *ingenuity* – inventiveness

Source information

Total text word count: 655 words

Text 1: Charlotte Brontë, A visit to the Crystal Palace, 1851. *The Brontës' Life and Letters*, by Clement Shorter (1907)

Text 2: The British Library; www.bl.uk/discovering-literature

PRACTICE PAPER 1: TEXT 1

SECTION A

Reading

Read Text 1 below and then answer Questions 1–3 on the Question Paper.

This is an extract from a pamphlet written in 1853 about 'ragged schools', which were charities set up to provide free education to poor children in 19th-century Britain.

Ask your friends to take you to see a Ragged School. There you will find poor children who have nobody at home to take care of them, or to teach them anything that is good, [children] whose wicked parents teach them to lie and steal, and who beat them if they come home without having stolen something. How would *you* like to be thus treated? Or to be turned out of doors on a bitterly cold night, when the nipping frost benumbed you, or when pitiless snow-storms and pelting rain fell 5

10

upon you? You would, I hope, be sorry if even your dog had to stay out on such a night! But just remember, that when you are going to your nice, warm, comfortable beds, after having plenty of good food and clothing, before lying down in peace and comfort, that there are hundreds of poor children who either have no home to go to, or such a home as you would fear to enter; that many pass the night under arches, or on the steps of doors – poor unhappy little beings! Oh, when you pray for yourselves, and ask God to bless your [family] then do not forget to ask Him also to help the poor outcasts. 15

PRACTICE PAPER 1: TEXT 2

Read Text 2 below and answer Questions 4–6 on the Question Paper.

In this extract from his journal published in 1884, a clergyman describes the living conditions of people living in a poor district of London.

THE Great Wild Street District of St. Giles-in-the-Fields is bounded on the east by Lincoln's-Inn-Fields and on the west by Drury Lane.

Fourpenny lodging-houses abound in the district, and it is full of other dwellings which are not half so comfortable even as fourpenny lodging-houses. Large families may still be found herding together in dark underground cellars, not fit for pigs to live in, or in stifling garrets[1] in which a tall man could   5
hardly stand upright. No matter how many families may be living in a house, the staircase is never lighted after the miserable glimmer of daylight has disappeared from its small dirty windows; and it is generally so badly constructed, so broken, and so narrow and winding towards the top, as to make it both difficult and dangerous for a stranger to feel his way up at night time.

The population of the district is mostly composed of the poorest of the poor – costermongers[2],   10
bricklayers' labourers, scavengers, dealers in rags and bones, chimney-sweeps, artisans who are always out of work, women and girls who earn a poor living in all sorts of ways, and a migratory people without visible means of living.

In this category, however, I do not include the people who live in the Peabody Buildings. But even here there are some very poor people, who find it a hard matter to pay the weekly rent and to get   15
bread enough to keep body and soul together.

The following facts will show how the poor live in this district.

A.B. is a scavenger earning 18s. a week. He has a wife and seven children. They live in a miserable back room with an open recess to it. Two of the children sleep in the same bed with their parents; the rest in a heap on the floor of the recess.   20

One day when I called upon this family to ascertain why the eldest boy had not been at my school on the previous Sunday, I found him in bed and asked what was the matter with him.

'Oh, sir,' replied the mother, 'there's nothing at all the matter with him, he's well enough. But all the same, he can't go out, and when any one knocks at the door, I make him jump into our bed.'

'But why should he not go out if he is well? And why should you make him jump into bed at this   25
time of day?'

'Well, sir, to tell you the truth the fact is, he's got no trousers to wear.'

Glossary

[1] *garret* – a top-floor or attic room.

[2] *costermonger* – a person who sells goods such as fruit and vegetables from a handcart in the street.

Source information

Total text word count: 655 words

Text 1: *Foodless, friendless, in our Streets; being a letter about Ragged Schools addressed to boys and girls* by Susanna Beever. Published 1853.

Text 2: *In the Slums: Pages from the Note-book of a London Diocesan Home Missionary* by the Rev. D. Rice-Jones. Published 1884.

Cut along the dotted lines and staple the texts together to make your own handy anthology. Make sure you keep it safe with your Revision Guide and Workbook.

TEXT 1

In this extract from the novel The Great Gatsby *by F. Scott Fitzgerald, a character named Nick is describing the frequent parties at his neighbour Gatsby's house.*

There was music from my neighbor's[1] house through the summer nights. On week-ends his Rolls-Royce became an omnibus[2], bearing parties to and from the city, between nine in the morning and long past midnight, while his station wagon scampered like a brisk yellow bug to meet all trains. And on Mondays eight servants including an extra gardener toiled all day with mops and scrubbing-brushes and hammers and garden-shears, repairing the ravages of the night before.   5

Every Friday five crates of oranges and lemons arrived from a fruiterer in New York—every Monday these same oranges and lemons left his back door in a pyramid of pulpless halves. There was a machine in the kitchen which could extract the juice of two hundred oranges in half an hour, if a little button was pressed two hundred times by a butler's thumb.   10

At least once a fortnight a corps of caterers came down with several hundred feet of canvas and enough colored[3] lights to make a Christmas tree of Gatsby's enormous garden. On buffet tables, garnished with glistening hors-d'œuvre[4], spiced baked hams crowded against salads of harlequin designs and pastry pigs and turkeys bewitched to a dark gold. In the main hall a bar with a real brass rail was set up, and stocked with gins and liquors and with cordials so long   15
forgotten that most of his guests were too young to know one from another.

By seven o'clock the orchestra has arrived—no thin five-piece affair but a whole pitful of oboes and trombones and saxophones and viols and cornets and piccolos and low and high drums. The last swimmers have come in from the beach now and are dressing upstairs; the cars from New York are parked five deep in the drive, and already the halls and salons   20
and verandas are gaudy with primary colors[5] and hair shorn in strange new ways and shawls beyond the dreams of Castile. The bar is in full swing and floating rounds of cocktails permeate the garden outside until the air is alive with chatter and laughter and casual innuendo[6] and introductions forgotten on the spot and enthusiastic meetings between women who never knew each other's names.   25

The lights grow brighter as the earth lurches away from the sun and now the orchestra is playing yellow cocktail music and the opera of voices pitches a key higher. Laughter is easier, minute by minute, spilled with prodigality[7], tipped out at a cheerful word. The groups change more swiftly, swell with new arrivals, dissolve and form in the same breath—already there are wanderers, confident girls who weave here and there among the stouter and more stable,   30
become for a sharp, joyous moment the center[8] of a group and then excited with triumph glide on through the sea-change of faces and voices and color under the constantly changing light.

1: *neighbor's* – American spelling of 'neighbour's'.
2: *omnibus* – bus.
3: *colored* – American spelling of 'coloured'.

4: *hors-d'œuvre* – small dish served at the start of a meal; starter, appetiser.
5: *colors* – American spelling of 'colours'.
6: *innuendo* – suggestive remark.

7: *prodigality* – excessive or extravagant spending.
8: *center* – American spelling of 'centre'.

Cut along the dotted lines and staple the texts together to make your own handy anthology. Make sure you keep it safe with your Revision Guide and Workbook.

TEXT 2

In this extract from a piece of travel writing, the writer explores what life is like for members of the crew on board a superyacht.

'Accès interdit[1],' says the sign on the Quai des Milliardaires in Antibes. Behind a barrier the superyachts rise like a skyline in white and royal blue. This is the smartest address in a smart town. Riff-raff are discouraged.

5 Still, nobody pays much attention as I wander up to the first of these beasts, the motor yacht Katara. It is thought to have cost around $300m. You don't spend that much on a boat not to have anyone notice. Crew in white shirts and khaki shorts swarm over its decks, making final preparations. Everything is immaculate. Glasses and cutlery are laid on tables. Sun-loungers are set out on the teak transom[2], towels rolled in tight cylinders. On the top deck a helicopter waits. It all gleams in the sunshine.

10 As I leave, I take a final wistful look up at the decking. It does look rather nice, I think, but then again that's the whole point. More than any other status symbol, these boats are the ultimate projections of global hyper-wealth: floating embassies of a world that is highly visible but impossible to touch. Unless you get a job on one, that is.

The work, for the majority of men and women, mostly consists of cleaning. Men are usually 15 deckhands, or 'deckies'. They clean the outside of the boat. Women are stewardesses, or 'stews'. They clean the inside of the boat. A big yacht can easily take two days to clean, and in the season it needs cleaning constantly. Toilets are cleaned with toothbrushes and cotton buds.

Culinary choices are only the start of the potential tensions on board. Compared with the 20 five-star hotel standard of the guest state-rooms, the crew accommodation is usually cramped and shared. Crew will wake up to serve breakfast and then stay until the last guest has gone to bed, meaning days can be up to 20 hours. There are no weekends at sea. On superyachts the owner is God, followed quickly by the captain and the guests.

Other tales are simply of excess. Every [crew member] has at least one ridiculous story and 25 it is impossible to tell which are true and which apocryphal[3]. The pig flown in from Denmark because someone wanted a hog roast. The dry cleaning sent to Paris. The artificial beach assembled on the back of one boat each day. The deckhands sent into the ocean to manually clear the area of jellyfish before a guest went swimming. Anything and everything procured on demand.

30 For the crew, life on board can be as enlightening as it is horrific at times. Somewhere between cutting cigars, pouring champagne and unblocking toilets, this is a job like few others.

1: accès interdit – French for 'access forbidden'.
2: transom – flat section at the back of a boat.
3: apocryphal – widely known but probably not true.

Source information

Total text word count: 919 words

Text 1: *The Great Gatsby* by F. Scott Fitzgerald. Published by Charles Scribner's Sons, 1925

Text 2: 'Sun, sea and silver service: what's it like crewing on a superyacht?' 7 September 2014 https://www.theguardian.com/lifeandstyle/2014/sep/07/crewing-on-superyachts-wealth-careers

PRACTICE PAPER 2: TEXT 1

SECTION A

Reading

Read Text 1 (fiction) below and then answer Questions 1–2 on the Question Paper.

In this extract from a novel, Pi describes the start of the sinking of the ship on which he, his family and their zoo animals are emigrating.

Inside the ship, there were noises. Deep structural groans. I stumbled and fell. I got up.
With the help of the handrails I went down the stairwell four steps at a time. I had gone down
just one level when I saw water. Lots of water. It was blocking my way. It was surging from
below like a riotous crowd, raging, frothing and boiling. Stairs vanished into watery darkness.
I couldn't believe my eyes. What was this water doing here? Where had it come from? I stood   5
nailed to the spot, frightened and incredulous and ignorant of what I should do next.
Down there was where my family was.

I ran up the stairs. I got to the main deck. The weather wasn't entertaining any more. I was very
afraid. Now it was plain and obvious: the ship was listing[1] badly. There was a noticeable incline
going from bow[2] to stern[3]. I looked overboard. The water didn't look to be eighty feet away.   10
The ship was sinking. My mind could hardly conceive it. It was as unbelievable as the moon
catching fire.

Where were the officers and the crew? What were they doing? Towards the bow I saw some
men running in the gloom. I thought I saw some animals too, but I dismissed the sight as
illusion crafted by rain and shadow. At all times the animals were kept confined to their cages.   15
These were dangerous wild animals we were transporting, not farm livestock.

The ship shook and there was that sound, the monstrous metallic burp. What was it? Was it the
collective scream of humans and animals protesting their oncoming death? Was it the ship itself
giving up the ghost? I fell over. I got to my feet. I looked overboard again. The sea was rising.
The waves were getting closer. We were sinking fast.   20

I clearly heard monkeys shrieking. Something was shaking the deck, a gaur – an Indian wild
ox – exploded out of the rain and thundered by me, terrified, out of control, berserk. I looked at
it, dumbstruck and amazed. Who in God's name had let it out?

I ran to the bridge. Up there was where the officers were, the only people on the ship who
spoke English, the masters of our destiny, the ones who would right this wrong. They would   25
explain everything. They would take care of my family and me. I climbed to the middle bridge.
There was no-one on the starboard side. I ran to the port side. I saw three men, crew members.
I fell. I got up. They were looking overboard. I shouted. They turned.

Glossary

[1] *listing* – tilting, tipping.

[2] *bow* – forward end; front end.

[3] *stern* – rear end.

PRACTICE PAPER 2: TEXT 2

Read Text 2 (non-fiction) below and answer Questions 3–4 on the Question Paper.

In this extract from a memoir, Doctor Washington Dodge describes the sinking and evacuation of the passenger ship, the Titanic.

I retired at 10.30 p.m. to be awakened about 11.40 by a violent jar[1]. I had the impression that the steamer had been struck on her side with sufficient force to move her bodily in a lateral direction. I hastily threw on a long overcoat and left my cabin to find a large number of passengers, all anxiously enquiring what had happened.

I went out on the deck and soon learned that we had run into ice. I heard a passenger state that   5
he saw the iceberg pass the stern[2] of the vessel to the height of the promenade deck, about 70 feet above the water. Walking rapidly forward, I saw the ice on the deck, and returned to my stateroom. Having been told there was no danger, and believing such from the general conduct of passengers and officers, I insisted that my family remain in bed and await developments.

I asked our steward what he had heard. He replied, 'The order has just come down for all   10
passengers to put on life preservers.' Rushing to my cabin I got my wife and son up and, allowing them to dress but partially, rushed them up on the boat deck. As boat number 3 was loaded, I placed them aboard. I watched this boat safely lowered to the water.

When boat 13 was lowered, someone pushed me from behind and shouted 'get in doctor'.
I climbed in and in a few moments the boat was filled. As we were lowered we were placed in   15
a perilous position which threated our destruction. As we neared the water our boat was being lowered directly into the immense volume of water thrown out from the ship's side by the condenser pump – a stream about 3 feet in diameter thrown with great force from the ship.
It would instantly have swamped our boat.

To add to our anxiety, boat 15 swung directly over our heads owing to the fact that the steamer had   20
settled several feet into the water at her bow. Both boats were being lowered when our loud cries of warning were heard and the lowering of both boats arrested. We had no officer in our boat to direct us but fortunately were able to disengage an oar, and with it push the bow of our boat, which overhung the threatening waters from the pump. We dropped into the water and were at once swept away from the steamer's side by great force of water.   25

The ocean being as calm as the waters of a smooth flowing river, we rowed off. We observed the closing incidents, the gradual submergence of the ship. The final extinguishment suddenly of all her lights. The final plunge downward as a shooting star fell from the zenith[3] nearly to the horizon.

Glossary

[1] *jar* – physical shock.

[2] *stern* – rear end.

[3] *zenith* – highest point in the sky.

Source information

Total text word count: 900 words

Text 1: *The Life of Pi* by Yann Martel. Published by Canongate, 2003.

Text 2: Washington Dodge, 1912. https://www.gilderlehrman.org

Answers

Where an exemplar answer is given, this is not necessarily the only correct response. In most cases there is a range of possible responses.

Exam skills

1 Exams explained: Paper 1

1 19th-century non-fiction texts.
2 1 hour 10 minutes.
3 One.

2 Exams explained: Paper 2

1 Contemporary texts and imaginative writing.
2 Six.
3 One.
4 45 minutes.

3 Planning your exam time

1 80 marks for each paper.
2 40 marks for each section.

Reading

4 Reading questions: an overview

1 Paper 1.
2 Any three from: prose fiction and literary non-fiction, such as novels, autobiographies, biographies, memoirs, letters, speeches and travel writing.
3 Any three from: crime, horror, science fiction, romance, satire.

5 Skimming for the main idea

Sample answer:

The main idea of the article is that a mother misses her child who has grown into a young man, and wishes she had appreciated day-to-day life more when he was a child.

6 Annotating the texts

While <u>Bath</u> is running, Ma gets <u>Labyrinth</u> and <u>Fort</u> down from the top of <u>Wardrobe</u>. We've been making Labyrinth since I was two, <u>she's</u> all toilet roll insides taped together in tunnels that twist lots of ways. Bouncy Ball loves to get lost in the Labyrinth and hide, I have to call out to <u>him</u> and shake <u>her</u> and turn her sideways and upside down before <u>he</u> rolls out, whew.

- Capitalised nouns for household items/toys – they have become names, friends, personification.
- Pronouns she and he used for inanimate objects.
- Long sentences, childlike language – suggests the narrator is young.

7 Explicit information and ideas

1 Any three from: voice, what we look like, how we walk, height.
2 At least fifty.
3 A good memory.

8 Implicit information and ideas

Sample answer:

1 Dickens went to observe the crowd watching an execution at Horsemonger-lane.
2 His disgust at the murderers and the gallows is overridden by his disgust of the gathered crowds.

9 The writer's viewpoint

Sample answer:

The repetition of 'idiot' emphasises the writer's point and ensures it is understood by the reader. Its repeated use reinforces the growing intensity of the insult.

10 Inference

Sample answer:

Hendrich is an old man who values his privacy: he lives in a house 'behind high fences and walls and hedges'. He is also presented as a perfectionist: 'even the trees looked perfect to the point of sterile.'

11 Connotations

Words	Connotations
red	danger, blood, anger
skull	death, danger, fear
lion	brave, strong, ruler

12 P–E–E paragraphs

Sample answers:

- **Point**: The writer is clearly disgusted by the reaction of the crowd to an already disturbing and gruesome public event.
- **Evidence**: This is revealed by the adjective in the lines 'before the atrocious bearing, looks and language, of the assembled spectators'.
- **Explanation**: This description of the crowd overrides the writer's initial reaction to the execution itself and the crime committed. The writer is making the clear point that this should not be a public event and those that choose to watch are as repulsive as the criminals, crime and punishment.

You can include more than one piece of evidence to back up a more fully developed point. Strong answers might also vary the order in which the point, the evidence and the explanation appear, but all of these elements should still be present.

13 Word classes

1   For as long as I can ⟨remember,⟩ all I've ⟨wanted⟩ to ⟨do⟩ is ⟨play.⟩ It doesn't ⟨matter⟩ what <u>position</u> I'⟨m playing⟩ in, what the <u>weather</u>⟨'s⟩ like or who the <u>opponent</u> ⟨is⟩ if you ⟨give⟩ me a <u>chance</u> to ⟨play⟩, that⟨'s⟩ what I'⟨m going⟩ to ⟨do⟩.
2   Sample answer:
The golden bread popped cheerily out of the toaster. The cereal crackled as the cool milk filled the bowl to the brim. The eggs spluttered and splattered loudly as the yolks oozed into the red-hot pan.

14 Figurative language

Sample answers:

Metaphor: Finishing school starts a new chapter in my life.

Simile: He was as cold as ice.

Personification: The sun smiled down on me.

15 Creation of character

Sample answer:

Gatsby is a wealthy and flamboyant man famed for throwing lavish parties.

16 Creation of atmosphere

1   The writer uses repetition of the word 'strange' to reinforce his confusion.
The writer uses themes of place, distance and movement to highlight the change and speed of time. He personifies time with 'jump' and 'hit' forcing the reader to consider the link between our past and present.
2   It is a reflective, questioning tone.

17 Whole text structure: non-fiction

Any three from:

* openings and conclusions
* paragraphs
* changes in tone
* positioning of facts, opinions and expert evidence.

18 Identifying sentence types

1   Minor sentence.
2   Multi-clause sentence (with coordinate clause).
3   Single-clause sentence.
4   Multi-clause sentence (with subordinate clause).

19 Commenting on sentence types

1   Short sentences/questions.
2   Long sentences.

3   Long and short sentences.
4   Volunteer today!

20 Synthesising two texts

1   (any one of) likewise, equally, as well, similarly.
2   (any one of) alternatively, on the other hand, in contrast, however.

21 Comparing ideas

Sample answer:

Both texts show how impressive the lives of the rich are compared to less wealthy people. For example, the detailed descriptions of the party setting by the narrator in *The Great Gatsby* gives the impression that he is in awe. In the travel writing, it is clearly stated from the outset that there is a division of 'worlds': 'This is the smartest address in a smart town. Riff-raff are discouraged.'

22 Comparing perspective

Sample answer:

In both texts, the writers use food to create impressions of the lives of the rich. However, they do it in very different ways. In Text 1, the writer describes vividly the different types of food that are served at the party. For example, he uses the metaphor that turkeys are 'bewitched to a dark gold'. Text 2 describes the 'immaculate' table settings and the 'excess' of a superyacht owner having a 'pig flown in from Denmark' for a hog roast. In Text 2, the emphasis is more the work of others in serving the owners and their guests than on the description of the food itself.

23 Comparing structure

Any three from:

* Openings and endings.
* Sequencing and cohesion.
* Paragraphs and the position/type of sentences.
* Changes in tone.

24 Comparing language

Any three from:

* Rhetorical language features.
* Tone, style and register.
* Words and phrases.
* Sentence forms.
* Connotations.
* Inferred meaning.
* Figurative language.

25 Evaluating a text

Answers could include:

* ideas: exhibition is impressive – 'mass of wealth' from all over the world

- events: people visit in large numbers – 'thirty thousand souls' – and walk through the exhibition dumb-struck – 'not one loud noise to be heard'
- themes: awe-inspiring exhibition – 'such a blaze of colour'; magic/supernatural to show how unusual and impressive it is.

26 Using evidence

Sample answer:

Throughout the text, the writer refers to precise times, days or weeks. For example: 'Every Friday five crates of oranges…'; 'At least once a fortnight a corps of caterers…'; and 'By seven o'clock the orchestra has arrived'.

'The lights grow brighter as the earth lurches away from the sun' signifies that the night is closing in.

'… sea-change of faces and voices and color under the constantly changing light' exemplifies the changing of the light through dusk, night and dawn.

Writing

27 Writing questions: an overview

1 Paper 1: transactional writing; Paper 2: imaginative writing.
2 One.
3 Both.

28 Writing for a purpose: transactional

Purpose: job application; audience: supermarket management; form: letter; tone: formal.

29 Ideas and planning: transactional

Example plan

Introduction: hundreds of channels, 24 hours a day, television can dominate.

Point 1: TV can be informative/educational.

Point 2: shared experience of high-quality drama, etc. (no different to theatre but cheaper and more accessible).

Counter-argument: some say it takes over our lives; they need to learn how to turn it off.

Conclusion: like anything, TV is good and bad; it depends on how it's used. Used carefully/selectively it can bring people together, entertain, inform and educate.

30 Writing for impact: transactional

Example plan

Introduction:
- Give overview of situation – young people have more exams to take than ever before, and schools are under pressure to continue raising grades; this creates extreme stress.

Subheading – How teenagers feel and how they act
- anxious and nervous about the exams
- confused about how to approach revision
- tired due to sleepless nights caused by worrying.

Subheading – What parents can do
- be supportive, not confrontational, if teenagers are rude
- provide healthy food and snacks
- help to write a revision timetable
- give praise when revision is done.

Subheading – Support available
- school year group team
- online revision websites
- older students or siblings.

Conclusion – Finally…
- plan some kind of celebration for results day
- ensure teenager knows they are loved, whatever the results.

31 Openings: transactional

Sample answers:

There is no point playing sport unless you play to win.

The majority of football games have a losing team.

Some things are better than winning.

32 Conclusions: transactional

1 Happy note.
2 Call to action.
3 Vivid image.
4 Thought-provoking question.
5 Warning.

33 Form: articles and reviews

Answers should include three differences between the formats, for example:
1 Reviews use figurative language; articles are more formal.
2 Reviews tend to give the writer's opinions more openly; articles are more likely to use quotations from other people as evidence and may give more than one point of view, or weigh up points of view.
3 Articles often use quotations from experts to make them seem factual and reliable; reviews are more emotive and personal.

34 Form: letters and reports

1 Letter.
2 Report.
3 Letter.

35 Form: speeches, emails and blogs

1D, 2C, 3E, 4A, 5B

36 Vocabulary for effect: transactional

Sample answers:

1 Fox-hunting is a totally barbaric activity where innocent wildlife suffers at the hands of privileged thugs.
2 Unnecessary plastic waste hangs around in the environment for decades, emitting hazardous particles into the atmosphere.
3 The measly amount that the lowest-paid workers receive is hardly enough to put food on the table.

37 Ideas and planning: imaginative

Sample answer:

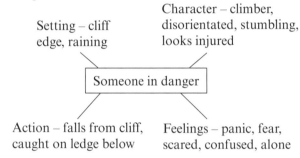

Setting – cliff edge, raining

Character – climber, disorientated, stumbling, looks injured

Someone in danger

Action – falls from cliff, caught on ledge below

Feelings – panic, fear, scared, confused, alone

38 Writing for an audience

Sample answers:

1 The audience is an older, adult reader. The writer is appealing to parents who have experience of this issue.
2 It doesn't have the appropriate tone and would not be acceptable to write in an exam. The student should use formal language to convey their argument and engage with the intended audience.
'Personally, I have never heard of anyone committing a violent action after playing a video game. That's not to say it hasn't happened, but it is not a common occurrence.'

39 Writing for a purpose: imaginative

Sample answers:

1 a Shivering beneath the clear blue sky
  b She radiated joy.
  c They yawned and fought to keep their eyes open.
  d The hairs on the back of his neck bristled.
2 a It's like a sauna.
  b It's an oven out there.
  c The sun hugged me.

40 Writing for impact: imaginative

Sample answers:

whispered, murmured, muttered

halted, arrested

crept, shuffled, dawdled

41 Structure: imaginative

Sample answer:

First person

Exposition: woke up – excited – going to a concert.

Complication: received message to say due to illness concert was cancelled.

Rollercoaster simile: surprise rising to anger then down to resignation.

Crisis: Mum says to stop sulking and help her at homeless shelter/meet mysterious stranger at homeless shelter.

Drag myself – show misery/reluctance through movements. Dialogue with stranger.

Resolution: start working at homeless shelter. Link improved mood with better weather.

42 Beginnings and endings: imaginative

Sample answers:

Dialogue: 'Who's there?' I shouted.

Senses to set the scene: Car headlights, like strobe lights in the sky, blinded me.

Mystery: When I left school that day, I had no idea of the events that would unfold.

Description of action: It bounded towards me. Snarling, unhindered by the undergrowth.

43 Vocabulary for effect: imaginative

Sample answers:

violent	cloudy	large	stopped	smiled
aggressive	milky	huge	impeded	beamed
cruel	opaque	immense	halted	grinned
vicious	hazy	mammoth	prevented	smirked

44 Paragraphs

Sample answer:

The provision of extra-curricular activities in our school is poor. There are few after-school sport or music groups, no drama club and no way of developing other valuable hobbies and interests within school. Students wishing to develop in areas away from the core curriculum have to attend private lessons or clubs. It is elitist to assume that everyone can afford to do this.

45 Linking ideas with adverbials

Sample answers:
1 A balanced diet will benefit your health. **Similarly**, exercise and plenty of sleep will help you maintain a healthy lifestyle.
2 I know I will be nervous **before** the exam. **Afterwards**, I expect to feel a huge sense of relief.
3 Playing games on a computer is boring. **Likewise**, doing homework on a computer is dull.
4 Our school has inadequate library resources. **Therefore**, students don't have access to new books and authors.
5 There are many reasons why lower speed limits should be introduced in towns, **chiefly** in areas close to schools and parks.
6 I like a wide variety of food, **for example** Thai, Mexican, Italian and Japanese cuisine.

46 Language for different effects 1

1 c	2 d	3 b
4 a	5 a	6 c

47 Language for different effects 2

Sample answers:
1 a You can encourage more people to recycle.
  b People can recycle cans, bottles and glass.
  c It's time to rise up for a recycling revolution.
2 a We can all find speaking in front of an audience overwhelming.
  b Speaking in public can be nerve-wracking, scary and intimidating.
  c Be calm, confident and concise.

48 Starting a sentence

Sample answers:

I was seven years old when we got a dog.

A tiny black, fluffy puppy arrived in a cardboard box.

After years of asking for a dog, my wish came true.

Crying with excitement, I held the tiny puppy in my arms.

Gentle, warm kisses smothered my face.

Shyly, the puppy emerged from the box.

Although she was with us now, I still felt like it was a dream.

49 Sentences for different effects

Sample answers:

At the heart of our community are those who contribute their time and effort to support others. Be a helper. Volunteer.

Building social networks, improving mental health, self-esteem, self-worth and life satisfaction are just some of the benefits of volunteering.

50 Formal and informal language

1 a I   b F   c I   d F

Sample answers:
2 a If you have any further queries, please do not hesitate to contact me.
  b Unfortunately, I am unavailable that day.

51 Commas

1 Florence, the most beautiful city in the world, has amazing museums and architecture.
2 Tom's present list included computer games, books, chocolate, football boots and a football.

52 Apostrophes and speech punctuation

1 I'll   don't   would've   They're
2 a 'I wouldn't like to go sky diving,' shivered Sam.
  b 'The hockey sticks aren't in the cupboard,' shouted Sohail. 'They're already on the field,' replied Mr Cook.

53 Colons, semicolons, brackets and dashes

1 The rainbow contains seven colours: red, orange, yellow, green, blue, indigo and violet.
2 a Toby loves pizza; Sohail does not.
3 a Shakespeare (who was also a prolific playwright) wrote over 150 sonnets.
  b Neil Armstrong (the first man on the moon) got his pilot's licence before he learned to drive a car.
4 a Marcus Rashford – who plays football for England – led a campaign against child poverty.
  The fair – which began in 1652 – is held each September.

54 Common spelling errors 1

They're the best band in the world.

I would like two cappuccinos please.

We were going to travel for a year but Covid-19 meant we couldn't go.

Our family tree can be traced back to the year 1365.

55 Common spelling errors 2

You're not going to believe what happened today. I was walking past the bus stop when out of nowhere, a learner driver drove off the road. He crashed into a wall. Thankfully the driver was ok, but I am sure it will have an effect on him. It's frightening to think how easily accidents can happen. I don't know whose fault it was – if anyone's. I think a tyre burst. Either way, I don't think he will have passed if he was taking his test.

56 Proofreading

The Covid-19 pandemic had a huge effect on everyone, but particularly young people. Lockdowns and periods of self-isolation meant that when they should have been experiencing life, the world outside of home was unavailable.